Along the Journey

The Story of S-Anon's First Forty Years

S-ANON
International
Family Groups

Library of Congress Control Number 2023920141
ISBN # 979-8-9874442-4-5
SAN: 255-0261

S-ANON
International
Family Groups

S-Anon Conference Approved Literature P-15
Printed in the United States of America.
Cover image used under license from Shutterstock.com.
First Edition: 2024

For information contact the S-Anon World Service Office:
S-Anon International Family Groups, Inc.
P.O. Box 17294
Nashville, TN 37217-0294
Phone: 615-833-3152 Toll-Free: 800-210-8141
Email: sanon@sanon.org
Website: www.sanon.org

God, grant me the serenity

To accept the things I cannot change,

Courage to change the things I can,

And wisdom to know the difference.

CONTENTS

ACRONYMS AND DEFINITIONS USED IN THIS BOOK

AA: Alcoholics Anonymous. AA is a Twelve Step recovery program for those who come together to stay sober and help other alcoholics to achieve sobriety.

AL-ANON: Al-Anon is a fellowship of relatives and friends of alcoholics who share their experience, strength, and hope in order to solve their common problems.

BOT: Board of Trustees. The BOT is a service arm of the World Service Conference. It exists as the legal entity for S-Anon International Family Groups, Inc. It is comprised of the Officers of the Board, Regional Trustees, Standing Committee Chairpersons, and the World Service Office Executive Director.

CAL: Conference Approved Literature. S-Anon recovery literature written by S-Anon members that has gone through member review and approval process to assure it represents the group conscience of the S-Anon fellowship. At the time of this printing, AA literature, Al-Anon literature, and SA literature, are also considered Conference Approved for use by S-Anon members. They contain helpful perspectives but are not expressly from the S-Anon point of view.

CBM: Conference Business Meeting. Prior to the formation of the World Service Conference, this was the group that discussed fellowship-wide business and made related decisions during business meetings at international conferences or conventions.

COC: Central Office Committee. This committee provided oversight to the S-Anon Central Office prior to the formation of the Board of Trustees.

FGC: Fellowship-wide Group Conscience. A decision-making process that can be undertaken in which all registered groups have a direct voice when an approved WSC motion calls for an FGC because the outcome will have a far-reaching effect on the S-Anon fellowship.

HP: Higher Power.

ICC: International Convention Committee. This is a standing committee of the Board of Trustees. The ICC provides guidance to international convention host planning committees in an effort to ensure that the international conventions proceed in accordance with the S-Anon Twelve Steps, Twelve Traditions, and Twelve Concepts of Service, and the BOT International Convention Committee Guidelines.

LC: Literature Committee. This is a standing committee of the Board of Trustees. Its purpose is to assure that every aspect of the S-Anon program of recovery is presented in adequate, comprehensive, and consistent written material. Literature includes books, pamphlets, leaflets, and other material that is reviewed and approved for distribution through the WSO to our members, friends, professionals, and to the world at large, via the S-Anon website.

SA: Sexaholics Anonymous. SA is a Twelve-Step recovery program for those who come together to achieve sexual sobriety.

S-Anews: S-Anon's quarterly newsletter published from 1992 to 2012. The newsletter, available as a subscription, was comprised of local, regional, and fellowship-wide news and updates, as well as member stories.

SIC: S-Anon International Committee. The SIC was the precursor to the service arm now known as the Board of Trustees.

SSSM: *S-Anon/S-Ateen Service Manual.* This manual is meant to serve as a member and group resource, grounded in S-Anon Twelve Traditions and Twelve Concepts of Service.

STD(s): Sexually Transmitted Disease(s).

WSC: World Service Conference. This is a forum where the issues and policies affecting all S-Anon and S-Ateen groups can be discussed and informed decisions can be made with all members of the fellowship represented. The WSC first met in 2004. WSC members consist of Area Delegates and BOT members.

WSCC: World Service Conference Committee. The WSCC is responsible for planning and facilitating the annual S-Anon World Service Conference.

WSO: World Service Office.

S-ANON PREAMBLE TO THE TWELVE STEPS

S-Anon is a fellowship of people who share their experience, strength, and hope with each other so that they may solve their common problems and help others to recover. The only requirement for membership is that there be a problem of sexaholism in a relative or friend. There are no dues or fees for S-Anon membership; we are self-supporting through our own contributions. S-Anon is not allied with any sect, denomination, politics, organization, or institution; does not wish to engage in any controversy; neither endorses nor opposes any causes. Our primary purpose is to recover from the effects upon us of another person's sexaholism and to help families and friends of sexaholics.

S-ANON TWELVE STEPS

1. We admitted we were powerless over sexaholism—that our lives had become unmanageable.
2. Came to believe that a Power greater than ourselves could restore us to sanity.
3. Made a decision to turn our will and our lives over to the care of God *as we understood Him.*
4. Made a searching and fearless moral inventory of ourselves.
5. Admitted to God, to ourselves, and to another human being the exact nature of our wrongs.
6. Were entirely ready to have God remove all these defects of character.
7. Humbly asked Him to remove our shortcomings.
8. Made a list of all persons we had harmed, and became willing to make amends to them all.
9. Made direct amends to such people wherever possible, except when to do so would injure them or others.
10. Continued to take personal inventory and when we were wrong promptly admitted it.
11. Sought through prayer and meditation to improve our conscious contact with God *as we understood Him*, praying only for knowledge of His will for us and the power to carry that out.
12. Having had a spiritual awakening as the result of these Steps, we tried to carry this message to others, and to practice these principles in all our affairs.

THE TWELVE STEPS OF ALCOHOLICS ANONYMOUS

1. We admitted we were powerless over alcohol—that our lives had become unmanageable. 2. Came to believe that a Power greater than ourselves could restore us to sanity. 3. Made a decision to turn our will and our lives over to the care of God *as we understood Him*. 4. Made a searching and fearless moral inventory of ourselves. 5. Admitted to God, to ourselves, and to another human being the exact nature of our wrongs. 6. Were entirely ready to have God remove all these defects of character. 7. Humbly asked Him to remove our shortcomings. 8. Made a list of all persons we had harmed, and became willing to make amends to them all. 9. Made direct amends to such people wherever possible, except when to do so would injure them or others. 10. Continued to take personal inventory and when we were wrong promptly admitted it. 11. Sought through prayer and meditation to improve our conscious contact with God *as we understood Him*, praying only for knowledge of His will for us and the power to carry that out. 12. Having had a spiritual awakening as the result of these Steps, we tried to carry this message to alcoholics, and to practice these principles in all our affairs.

S-ANON TWELVE TRADITIONS

1. Our common welfare should come first; personal progress for the greatest number depends upon unity.
2. For our group purpose there is but one authority—a loving God as He may express Himself in our group conscience. Our leaders are but trusted servants—they do not govern.
3. The relatives of sexaholics, when gathered together for mutual aid, may call themselves an S-Anon Family Group, provided that, as a group, they have no other affiliation. The only requirement for membership is that there be a problem of sexaholism in a relative or friend.
4. Each group should be autonomous, except in matters affecting another group or S-Anon or SA as a whole.
5. Each S-Anon Family Group has but one purpose: to help families of sexaholics. We do this by practicing the Twelve Steps of S-Anon, by encouraging and understanding our sexaholic relatives, and by welcoming and giving comfort to the families of sexaholics.
6. Our S-Anon Family Groups ought never endorse, finance, or lend our name to any outside enterprise, lest problems of money, property, and prestige divert us from our primary spiritual aim. Although a separate entity, we should always cooperate with Sexaholics Anonymous.
7. Every group ought to be fully self-supporting, declining outside contributions.
8. S-Anon Twelfth Step work should remain forever non-professional, but our service centers may employ special workers.
9. Our groups, as such, ought never be organized; but we may create service boards or committees directly responsible to those they serve.

10. The S-Anon Family Groups have no opinion on outside issues; hence our name ought never be drawn into public controversy.

11. Our public relations policy is based on attraction rather than promotion; we need always maintain personal anonymity at the level of press, radio, TV, and films. We need guard with special care the anonymity of all S-Anon and SA members.

12. Anonymity is the spiritual foundation of all our Traditions, ever reminding us to place principles above personalities.

S-ANON TWELVE CONCEPTS OF SERVICE

S-Anon's Twelve Concepts of Service illustrate that Twelfth Step work can be accomplished on a broad scale. The Concepts are guidelines for the World Service Office staff, the Board of Trustees, standing committees, and World Service Conference members to relate to each other and to groups.

1. The ultimate responsibility and authority for S-Anon world services belongs to the S-Anon groups.
2. The S-Anon Family Groups have delegated complete administrative and operational authority to their Conference and its service arms.
3. The Right of Decision makes effective leadership possible.
4. Participation is the key to harmony.
5. The Rights of Appeal and Petition protect minorities and assure that they be heard.
6. The Conference acknowledges the primary administrative responsibility of the trustees.
7. The trustees have legal rights while the rights of the Conference are traditional.
8. The Board of Trustees delegates full authority for routine management of the S-Anon Headquarters to its executive committees.
9. Good personal leadership at all service levels is a necessity. In the field of world service the Board of Trustees assumes the primary leadership.

10. Service responsibility is balanced by carefully defined service authority and double-headed management is avoided.

11. The World Service Office is composed of an executive director and staff members.

12. The spiritual foundation for S-Anon's world services is contained in the General Warranties of the Conference, Article 12 of the Charter.

The General Warranties of the Conference

In all its proceedings the World Service Conference of S-Anon shall observe the spirit of the Traditions:

1. that only sufficient operating funds, including an ample reserve, be its prudent financial principle;
2. that no Conference member shall be placed in unqualified authority over other members;
3. that all decisions be reached by discussion, vote, and whenever possible, by unanimity;
4. that no Conference action ever be personally punitive or an incitement to public controversy;
5. that though the Conference serves S-Anon, it shall never perform any act of government; and like the fellowship of S-Anon which it serves, it shall always remain democratic in thought and action.

(The Twelve Concepts of Service reprinted and adapted with permission of Al-Anon World Services, Inc. Permission to reprint and adapt the Con- cepts does not imply that Al-Anon is affiliated with this program. Al-Anon is a program of recovery from the effects of alcoholism. Use of this mate- rial in connection with programs which are patterned after Al-Anon, but which address other problems, does not imply otherwise.) S-Anon's Twelve Concepts of Service were formally adopted and approved at the first annual S-Anon World Service Conference, January 2004.

ACKNOWLEDGMENTS

A Power greater than ourselves has guided our fellowship and this project, not only in ways we have acknowledged, but also in ways we have not yet discovered.

We wish to express sincere and heartfelt gratitude to our earliest members. These brave women and men dared to believe that healing from the effects of another's sex addiction is possible. Their courage and strength provided the foundation on which S-Anon stands today.

This book was made possible because of the kindness, generosity of spirit, and patience of our early members. Their honesty and willingness to share their recovery stories enlightened us about their hopes and struggles, as they charted the course of S-Anon becoming an established Twelve Step program.

We are grateful to the countless members who thoughtfully answered questionnaires, filled in gaps, or participated in phone interviews. With your help, we were able to present a fuller, more accurate picture of our collective journey.

Thank you to the many members who spent hours, months, and even years sorting, transcribing, and organizing nearly one thousand documents. All these documents were instrumental in unraveling the compelling story of the formation and development of the S-Anon program. The support provided by the S-Anon World Service Office (WSO) staff was invaluable. They shared their resources and provided a place to work. Without their help, we would not have been able to piece together this story. S-Anon truly is a "we" program.

We owe a special thanks to Alcoholics Anonymous and Al-Anon, who have preceded us in recovery. Their Twelve Steps, Twelve Traditions, and Twelve Concepts of Service are gifts as well as blueprints for our healing and growth.

ABOUT THE DOCUMENTATION

This book is based on the memories of many S-Anon members, numerous documents, and dedicated research. Some of the information came from unsigned documents, along with hundreds of letters, notes, transcribed recordings, business and committee meeting minutes, programs and flyers from recovery events, and questionnaires. We also relied on the S-Anews, a quarterly newsletter published from 1989 to 2012. All of these helped bring to life the history of the S-Anon fellowship.

Occasionally, contradictions were found between the many documents and a member's recall of dates and events. Every attempt was made to cross check information. Whenever possible, we conducted interviews, mostly with our earliest members. We strove to be accurate and objective when telling this story. Although our early members faced their individual struggles, they were able to put aside differences and learn to work together for a common cause: to help each other recover from the effects that another person's sex addiction had on their lives.

INTRODUCTION

In the winter of 1983 in Simi Valley, California, six women came together seeking a solution to their common problem of being affected by another person's sexual behavior. They made a commitment to support each other, and out of their desperation and by working together, they found the strength and received the guidance they needed to create the S-Anon program. This book celebrates the solutions they found in their S-Anon journey and describes many of their struggles along the way. It also provides insight into how members began to apply the spiritual principles of the S-Anon program to their personal lives with the help of the S-Anon Twelve Steps, Twelve Traditions, and Twelve Concepts of Service.

As far back as 1988, the S-Anon fellowship recognized the need to document its history. Discussions continued, and an Archives Committee of the Board of Trustees was eventually formed in 2000 to start organizing, preserving, and archiving our past. We have found it humbling to know that we have been guided by a power greater than ourselves throughout our S-Anon journey.

Along the Journey gives us an opportunity to take a thorough and objective look at our fellowship's development. It invites us to recognize our many strengths as well as admit our shortcomings. Our Fourth Step states: "Made a searching and fearless moral inventory of ourselves." Studying and learning about the past and present can increase our understanding of the principles of our program and further our spiritual growth.

This book provides insight into the beginnings of the S-Anon program, describes historical events, includes stories of challenges and progress, and documents the growth of our fellowship. There are questions for reflection throughout each chapter. Quotes from early members, speaking from their personal recollections, are also included. We hope this book will inspire your personal recovery and provide discussion topics for use in S-Anon meetings.

In the early chapters, which discuss our history before S-Anon Conference Approved Literature (CAL) existed, quotations or mention of literature which is not S-Anon CAL are cited to ensure historical accuracy. Quotes from these sources do not indicate Conference Approval of these publications, nor do they constitute endorsement of or imply S-Anon's affiliation with any outside entities.

While compiling historical information, we recognized some interesting patterns. A common thread among many of the earliest members was that they were women, married to sex addicts, looking for a solution to save their marriages. S-Anon began from that perspective. This is evident in some of the literature we use even to this day. Current demographics, however, show that S-Anon now attracts a broader range of people. S-Anon and S-Ateen are available to anyone seeking help and hope, including those who are single, divorced, married, of any gender identity or sexual orientation, teenagers, parents, adult children of sex addicts, extended family members, acquaintances, and coworkers. We welcome anyone who has been affected by another's sex addiction or sexual behavior.

We hope this book will help you reflect on your own one-day-at-a-time journey to serenity, dignity, and emotional growth.

CHAPTER ONE

"The New Alcoholism"
What It Used to be Like

Taking a brief look at some of the social and cultural values prior to the existence of Twelve Step recovery for sex addicts and their families helps us understand the challenges faced by the pioneers of the S-Anon program.

During the 1960s and 1970s, many of the long-accepted social norms in the United States were challenged in a number of ways. The women's liberation movement, the growing civil rights movement, and the turmoil surrounding the Vietnam War brought ground-breaking cultural changes. This time period also included the peace movement and the sexual revolution.

By then, many people had heard of alcoholism and understood it to be a disease. However, there was much controversy among physicians and mental health professionals as to whether sex addiction was a disease, an actual addiction, or a moral issue. Various theories and possible solutions were proposed to address these problems.

Some professionals believed sexually "excessive" behavior was a result of alcohol or drug addiction. They thought the inappropriate sexual behavior would go away once the drug or alcohol addiction was under control. Some thought it was nothing more than having a high sex drive. Others considered the problem to be a lack of self-control. The media soon became interested in this controversial subject, and articles that called attention to the problem began to appear in newspapers, books, and magazines.

A few publications began to appear in bookstores. Most were written for the sex addict, but there were some for family members as well. Some people read everything they could find to help understand and try to "fix" the problem. As more information about sexual addiction became available, the focus remained primarily on the addict. Spouses of addicts were often portrayed as victims. Other family members or friends were seldom considered to need help.

> The first time I ever read or heard about sexual addiction was in a book they were selling at another meeting I attended. It was 1978 or 1979. A friend bought the book and then loaned it to me. There were two chapters that described sexual compulsion. I read two paragraphs to my husband one night and his face went white. He said, "Is that in black and white?"
>
> Early S-Anon member, questionnaire

Public and personal fear and concern based on family experiences, religious beliefs, and rumors added confusion and raised many questions regarding sex addiction. Health and safety concerns intensified the alarming and dangerous ramifications of this disease, both for the sex addicts and their partners. The early 1980s brought HIV and AIDS awareness and raised fears about an increase in cases of other sexually transmitted diseases (STDs).

The idea of such a thing as sex addiction was starting to gain acceptance among medical and other professionals. In the October 10, 1984, edition of the "Science Times" section of the *New York Times,* there was an article about how certain excessive sexual behavior could be seen as an addiction, similar to the excesses seen in other addictions such as alcoholism. As of the date of this publication, there are still differing opinions in the medical and mental health communities about whether or not to define sex addiction as a disease.

During the 1980s, the therapeutic community began using the labels "co-addiction" and "co-dependence." The recovery community had already recognized the impact of addiction on family and friends. Society in general was beginning to acknowledge that these issues affected more than just the spouse or partner.

Throughout S-Anon's formative years, people often used those clinical terms to describe their relationship with the addict. Subsequently, those terms were used in our first publication, "The Co-Addict's Checklist," as well as some other early readings. Many early meetings handed out a list of "helpful" outside literature, including books on co-dependency. Members' stories and articles in the *S-Anews* frequently included this terminology. As we became more sensitive to how this language could be seen as endorsement of specific therapies for S-Anon members, clinical language in our literature and the use of outside literature were discontinued.

General attitudes of that era tended to disregard the predicament of families and friends of sex addicts. The idea that this was a family disease was not considered or discussed. The impact that the effects of sexual addiction could have on family, friends, or others was, and still is, difficult for much of society to grasp.

This was a disturbing time for family members and friends of sex addicts. Some people grasped at any sources they could find for help, including Twelve Step programs, counseling, and other therapies. The threat of becoming infected with HIV, AIDS, herpes, and other STDs was real. It was difficult for many of them to seek help or find support. Some suffered deep despair and loneliness whether or not they stayed in a relationship with a sex addict.

> It took me many months to get the courage to go for my first HIV test. At that time, the counselor told me I was in a very low-risk category since I was heterosexual and monogamous, even though I had no idea of the nature of my husband's sexual behavior.
>
> I was told to insist on condoms. I felt shame when my husband said I should never doubt him, and he refused to discuss the subject. I got tested every six months and continued to hope and wish my husband was either monogamous or practicing safe sex. Eventually I contracted gonorrhea.
>
> Today I do not know what he is doing. What I do know is that I don't have sex without condoms. I truly believe that my Higher Power gave me one last chance when I contracted gonorrhea. I learned that what I don't know most assuredly can hurt me. Dying for love is only romantic in the movies.
>
> S-Anon member, *S-Anews*, Summer 1992

"Dear Abby" (a syndicated newspaper advice column) was a helpful source of information for the general public. The following response to a letter from a woman impacted by the sexual behavior of her spouse brought many calls and letters to the S-Anon office.

> From *Dear Abby,* September 1, 1997:
>
> Dear Feeling Used: You must love your husband very much to have remained with him through all the tribulations you describe. Sex addiction is nothing new. I have known about it since the early 1980's, when I first learned of the existence of a 12-step fellowship of sex addicts called Sexaholics Anonymous (SA).
>
> Operating in conjunction with SA are the S-Anon International Family Groups—12-Step fellowships of people who have been affected by the sexual addiction of a family member or friend. A program such as this could provide comfort and direction for you.
>
> S-Anon members are wives, husbands, children, parents, siblings, friends, and even co-workers of sex addicts. Banding together in a program based on the principles of Alcoholics Anonymous, they work to resolve their common problems and to help others recover from the effects of another's sexual addiction.[1]

---

[1] As seen in DEAR ABBY by Abigail Van Buren a.k.a. Jeanne Phillips and founded by her mother Pauline Phillips.

Chapter One

• • •

Up for Discussion…

1. What is my understanding of how someone's sex addiction affects partners, family members, and friends?

2. In what ways do I see the media influencing public perception regarding those who have been affected by sexual addiction?

3. Did the media, a health care worker, or someone else play a part in my finding S-Anon?

4. How have I been affected by what I perceive others may think about my circumstances and the relationship choices I have made?

5. What has been my personal experience with understanding sex addiction as a disease?

• • •

DEVELOPMENT OF A TWELVE STEP PROGRAM

Just as with other Twelve Step programs, the formation of S-Anon took many twists and turns before there was a solid start. This bumpy beginning is something we can now celebrate. People made an effort to come together to heal from the effects of sexual addiction in spite of shame, confusion, and isolation.

By 1981, Sexaholics Anonymous was organized. Whenever they gathered for meetings or conferences, there were usually a few spouses along as well. Two wives of sex addicts met informally during an early SA conference. Two wives in western Ohio also held a meeting in 1981. Between 1981 and 1984, a few S-Anon meetings formed independently, without benefit of Conference Approved Literature (CAL) or a central office. It was as though a spark of an idea began to glow in various parts of the United States and Europe.

The growth and development of S-Anon was inconsistent and not well documented during this time. Communication was limited, and sharing the S-Anon message was a challenge. Due to a lack of strong organization and support, records were not maintained or preserved. Geographical distance between members was another challenge. There were no fax machines, personal computers, or email at that time. The primary methods of communication included mailing letters, making costly long-distance telephone calls, and talking face-to-face at infrequent events.

Then something notable happened in December of 1983. A group of SA members gathered for their third National Conference in Simi Valley, CA. Six women, all wives of SA members, were present at the conference. Four had come from out of state. They came together, desperate to find help for the problem of living with active sexual addiction and to heal from the wounds of past betrayals. They wept and comforted each other, sharing their deepest pain and fear. They were no longer alone, having found others who understood what they were going through.

There was no formal agenda when the six women gathered in Simi Valley. One by one, they shared their stories with the group. They talked about the nature of their betrayal and expressed their hurt and anger toward the sexaholic, their bewilderment when facing the reality of broken marriage vows, the confusion of having their self-identity shattered, and even their anger toward their Higher Power. Their experience was the beginning of S-Anon, which would gradually expand and grow to offer help to multitudes who were still suffering.

At least three of those women may have planned in advance to meet that weekend. Two of them were from Phoenix, Arizona, and attended without their spouses. We believe this event was significant because it indicated a sincere desire to meet with other people who understood what they were going through. One of the women from Phoenix had prior experience with other Twelve Step programs. Her presence demonstrated how important it was to her for family and friends of sex addicts to have their own program for the help and support they needed.

At that December conference, Sexaholics Anonymous struggled with handling its own growing organization and responding to a deluge of inquiries generated by media articles. A number of those letters were from family members of sex addicts asking for help, which the SA Central Office was unprepared to answer. They asked the six women if they would be willing to respond to those letters.

Accepting that request placed an urgent and heavy burden squarely on those few individuals, leaving them wondering how to respond. An energetic discussion followed about how they should answer the letters, as well as how to help people start meetings. They discovered a common desire to reach out and share recovery with the people who had written for help.

The two women from Phoenix had started a local meeting, and they believed that members who attended the new meeting would be willing to help. One of the two women volunteered to become the mail response contact person. The other woman offered to help get S-Anon representation at the next SA conference. Another of the six attendees, who was from the West Coast, was elected as the first S-Anon Committee Chairperson. She agreed to set up a system of mail and phone contacts as a way to carry the S-Anon message of recovery.

By referencing a copy of a flyer from the newly formed Codependents of Sex Addicts (COSA) fellowship and being well informed about Al-Anon literature, they discussed what to "borrow" to create an S-Anon brochure. The decision was made to adopt "The Dilemma" from Adult Children of Alcoholics (ACOA, today known as ACA), and create a draft of the "Co-Addict's Checklist" questions.

It's official!

The actions taken that weekend by those six women helped the S-Anon fellowship to take root. Their contributions, along with those of many others during those early years, were instrumental in establishing the fellowship we benefit from today. More than thirty years later, in July 2014, a motion was brought to the World Service Conference to approve S-Anon's founding date as December of 1983. The motion unanimously passed.

• • •

Up for Discussion…

1. Was I aware of the history of the S-Anon program? In what ways can I relate the fellowship's history to my own challenges in recovery? Has my group considered asking an "old timer" to speak about their experiences of early S-Anon?

2. Do I know who started my local meeting and what it was like for them?

3. Would I consider documenting the history of S-Anon meetings in my area?

4. In what ways do I consider S-Anon as a worldwide fellowship rather than as simply my home group?

5. How have I benefitted from fellowship in the S-Anon program?

CHAPTER TWO

Meetings Sprout Up

Tracing the roots of S-Anon meetings is essential for us to understand the story of our fellowship. As information about S-Anon began to spread in the mid-1980s, meetings sprouted up across the United States. Some newspapers provided contact information about meetings. Sometimes people found their way to a conference or other recovery event. Therapists would occasionally recommend S-Anon to their clients. As more people realized they were not alone in their suffering from the effects of another's sex addiction, they found courage to seek a solution and start meetings in their local areas. It was a miracle that a power greater than ourselves brought us together.

The evolution of S-Anon meetings has been a story of both successes and challenges; while some meetings grew, others closed. There are several reasons why some meetings do not thrive. Some members stop attending when their relationship with the sexaholic dissolves, not realizing the benefits of staying in the program for themselves. They change jobs, move to different areas, or have other life-changing events, and they might stop attending meetings. The challenge of confronting their own fear, shame, and guilt about the effects that sex addiction has had on their lives may be too much for some of them, or they simply are not ready to attend meetings regularly. Meetings might also dissolve when the S-Anon Traditions are not followed, which may create resentments or place personalities above principles.

The first documented meeting was attended by two wives of sexaholics in western Ohio in 1981. Details of where they met, who they were, or what happened were not documented. Around that same time, a woman living in Los Angeles, California, sought help in Al-Anon. She found that the Al-Anon program did not adequately address the challenges of living with sex addiction and so decided to form a separate group.

In 1982 they gathered in one of their homes to start a meeting. They called themselves "S-Anon," adapting the name of Al-Anon. At some point they disbanded. Unfortunately, it was not possible to identify these women to hear their stories. Other S-Anon meetings began to form, but it took time for those sprouts to take root. The following is a glimpse of some of those early meetings.

• • •

1983

OKLAHOMA CITY, OKLAHOMA

After meeting an S-Anon member who was visiting from another state at an open A.A. meeting in Oklahoma City, Oklahoma, our first male member realized he needed help with his S-Anon problem. Since he did not have the benefit of a local meeting, he asked her to sponsor him. With her encouragement, he and one other member started the first S-Anon meeting in Oklahoma City. Although it had a few stops and starts, that same meeting still meets as of 2021.

> For a long time, I didn't want to have anything to do with you people. I came along to carry the baggage and to provide a little lip service support for my wife, who is a recovering sex addict. That was the only reason I was here.
>
> I can tell you some things have changed over the years. I can recount my beginning in S-Anon in May of 1983. Back then I felt like a token member of S-Anon, and I felt totally out of place being a male. Today I no longer feel like a token member; I am right where I am supposed to be.
>
> S-Anon Speaker, Unity Conference,
> Orange, California, January 4, 1995

This member participated in many areas of S-Anon service. He later served on the S-Anon International Committee (SIC), which preceded the S-Anon Board of Trustees, and helped obtain our first incorporation as a non-profit. The other member served by taking responsibility for the S-Anon office that was originally started in Arizona. She worked with others to improve the meeting format and literature. She participated at conferences and shared her recovery wherever and whenever she could.

PHOENIX, ARIZONA

In the latter part of 1983, two women started an S-Anon meeting in Phoenix. No further details about this meeting are known.

• • •

1984

SOUTHWEST AND SOUTHEAST

As the two Oklahoma City members were struggling to keep their meeting going, other meetings started in 1984. Two S-Anon members, one from the southeast and one from the southwest, began their individual searches for hope and help. They both became deeply involved in the formation of the fellowship as it grew and matured. They helped develop the organizational structure, participated in writing and editing literature, volunteered in planning recovery events, and carried the message at conventions, marathons, and retreats.

> When I came into S-Anon in 1984, there actually was a meeting already started in Nashville, Tennessee. There were two women, both from out of the general vicinity, who would come into the city to hold that meeting. I remember it was the three of us for a very long time.
>
> At some point, both of these people dropped out, and I found myself often alone in that meeting. It was April 14th—I remember because I had my taxes with me, in fact, and I was sitting there alone (again) on the top floor

of this church. I was really gnashing my teeth; I was so mad.

I was angry that there was no meeting, and I was sitting there wasting my precious time. Wouldn't you know it, I left my taxes there, and I had to go back the next day and retrieve them. I realized God was telling me something. Over time S-Anon in our area started to grow.

S-Anon member, recorded speaker

Before I attended my first S-Anon conference in June 1984, I had begun to organize an S-Anon meeting in Tucson, Arizona. I had been attending Al-Anon and listening to the members share. When I heard someone who sounded as if she was dealing with the effects of someone's sex addiction, I would approach her.

Eventually I met a woman who is still my friend decades later. She and I organized S-Anon in Tucson. We met first in a church and later in a local hospital. We timed it to coincide with the sex addicts' meeting. For a long time, it was just the two of us, but eventually it grew.

When some therapists in town became interested in sex addiction, we told them about the meeting. On May 5, 1985, we got a big story in the local newspaper. It was on the first page of the entertainment section and in huge letters it was titled "Sexaholic: Addict of Infidelity." It led to a lot of people joining SA and S-Anon.

S-Anon member,
Archives Committee questionnaire

GERMANY

In October 1984, a person from Germany heard about S-Anon during a stay in the United States. They shared this information with the staff of a hospital near Karlsruhe (southern Germany) and started a meeting in that hospital.

Several months later, four members started an S-Anon meeting in Karlsruhe in a "steeple room" that a church agreed to provide. These four members were familiar with the framework of Twelve Step programs. The only literature available was a flyer from the U.S. written in English. One of them understood English and orally translated it into German. They soon made the first written translation of S-Anon literature.

> The group in Karlsruhe, founded in 1985, continues to have regular meetings. One original founding member is still active in this group along with several long-term members.
>
> Membership in S-Anon crosses all borders and provides a great sense of community. Regardless of everything that has happened, good and bad times, all members have contributed to the well-being of this small community.
>
> There are those who have stayed, those who are new, those who were with us for a short while, and those who have passed away. I'm grateful for this Twelve Step program with all its blessings, such as consolation, recovery, and spiritual healing.
>
> German S-Anon member

> My first experience with S-Anon was in May of 1985 in Germany. There were German-speaking S-Anon meetings, which I believe saved my life. They all understood, spoke, and wrote more English than I spoke and wrote German, that's for sure.
>
> We didn't understand everything each other was saying. My situation was probably nothing like theirs, but they felt the anger. They heard the self-pity, and they heard the self-justification, and they loved me anyway. They told me to keep coming back—I think. I'm pretty sure that's what they were saying.
>
> We just had a lot of questions and not many answers in those days. And yet the love of the fellowship, the

gathering with other people who had those experiences, was healing, whether or not we had all the answers. We didn't have to have all the answers. I'm really grateful for that experience. They were there when I needed somebody desperately.

American S-Anon member who lived in Germany

• • •

1985

LOS ANGELES, CALIFORNIA

A meeting began in West Los Angeles in February 1985. The woman who started this meeting was hurting and fearful, but her courage and perseverance were instrumental in helping S-Anon grow.

I was encouraged by my sponsor in another program and my psychiatrist to start a meeting. They said sexaholism is an addiction like alcoholism, only tied with a different ribbon.

Encouraged by the founder of Sexaholics Anonymous, I went to the church in West Los Angeles where SA met regularly to ask for a room in which to meet. I walked in with all my old childhood shame and humiliation. I could only say I needed space for the families and wives of the Saturday night group. I couldn't say sex addiction.

I waited for what seemed forever, and after a couple of weeks I got the approval. I took my Step study from another program and substituted words. I also had some tapes on how to work a Twelve Step program that were very helpful.

The first meeting took place in February 1985. A newcomer, who used to wait in the car for her spouse, brought her baby, and we put him on a blanket in the middle of the floor while we had a meeting. At the second meeting a member came from Bozeman, Montana. She said to me, "This meeting will grow if you stay in recovery and not in the problem." That got hard wired in my head, and we started to grow.

S-Anon member

• • •

1986

PORTLAND, OREGON

Our first meeting in Portland, Oregon, was very small–one other woman and me. We met at a retreat center in Portland, not far from my home. This was very early 1986. There was no format. A lot of pain was shared between us. We both had some Al-Anon background, so that helped quite a bit.

S-Anon member, international convention recording

ROCHESTER, NEW YORK

In Rochester, New York, during the spring of 1986, Higher Power (HP) brought four women together after we were in a day program for recovering codependency. Since our husbands had the disease of sex addiction, we had a common bond. We learned that there was a program for people like us.

To be truthful, Higher Power was the one who started our meeting in Rochester. We were just His instruments. We began meeting in one of our homes and soon learned that if we were to help others and recover ourselves, we needed one of those church basements. Again, HP orchestrated all the details. I am a grateful member of our group and so happy to give back what has been given to me.

S-Anon member, Rochester, New York

• • •

1987

MACON, GEORGIA

I first began attending a meeting in a counseling suite in Atlanta, Georgia. It was not S-Anon, but it was a group for friends and family members of sex addicts.

Sometime in 1987 I contacted the S-Anon Office, and they sent me some material. Soon after, I met another woman who lived in my area, and the two of us started an S-Anon meeting at my house in Fort Valley, Georgia. We used a format from S-Anon and some other influences. A few months later, we began meeting in Macon, Georgia, at a private psychiatric hospital. We later relocated to two different churches. That meeting continued until sometime in the mid-1990s when we decided to close it.

S-Anon member, questionnaire and personal reflections

WARREN, MICHIGAN

I attended my first S-Anon meeting in August of 1987. I went to the meeting only because my therapist said she would not continue to see me unless I went to an S-Anon meeting. One other newcomer also came to the meeting that night. Two women had just started the meeting the previous month. Our meeting space was actually my therapist's office. She didn't see clients on Mondays, so she let us use her office for our meeting. Although we outgrew the original meeting space and we changed locations, this Monday meeting in Warren is still my home group today. In 1987 there was no S-Anon literature other than a pamphlet called the "Co-Addict's Checklist." We had no old-timers to share their wisdom with us, so we said we were 'the blind leading the blind.' That really didn't seem to matter because I was so relieved not to be alone in the problem anymore.

S-Anon member, personal reflections

• • •

1988

BALTIMORE, MARYLAND – WASHINGTON, D.C. AREA

My husband, a sexaholic, and I moved back to the States from Germany in 1988. In July that year, I went to my first convention in Rochester, NY. Conventions are very special to me. I felt safe and first saw some really sober S-Anon members that I could relate to…it's like the light went on.

I saw how devastating sex addiction had been to my life. Soon after returning home, we started the first S-Anon meeting in the Baltimore – Washington D.C. area. There were four of us that met in a church. People came and went.

S-Anon international convention speaker

By 1988, approximately 50 registered groups were meeting across the United States and Canada. Meetings frequently started up and disbanded. Sometimes it took a while before there were more than one or two members regularly attending the meetings. Other known meetings were located in Utah, Illinois, Montana, Ohio, Wisconsin, Kansas, Massachusetts, and Canada. A few states were fortunate to have more than one meeting.

• • •

1990'S AND FORWARD

In September 1996, a meeting started in Toronto, Ontario. Sometimes only two or three members would attend. Regardless of numbers, the meeting was always held as if the room was full. At other times, the meeting grew and was attended by as many as twenty members. Twenty-five years later, in 2021, this group is still meeting at the same time and location.

Eventually, courageous members made it possible for more S-Anon meetings to start. As progress in technology and communications expanded, online and telephone meetings became possible. The first online email meeting began in February 1997, and by November of that year a dozen members routinely participated. Guidelines were posted along with an anonymity statement. A member wanting to join would send an email request indicating how they qualified.

The S-Anon International Committee (SIC) discussed the online meeting in November 1997 and asked one of its founders to participate. They expressed concern that the group might get too large for one person to coordinate, that this service could become extremely time-consuming, and that an email meeting should not be a substitute for a face-to-face meeting.

This member agreed to work on guidelines and suggestions, while another member investigated writing an article for *S-Anews* (S-Anon's quarterly newsletter, published from 1992 to 2012). They also sought additional volunteers willing to become coordinators for the email meeting. An announcement was placed in the June 1998 *S-Anews* that anyone interested in the new email meeting should contact the Central Office. The email meeting closed in 2019.

Somewhere around 2007, a few S-Anon members from Chicago, Illinois, started a telephone meeting because several longtime members had moved out of the area, and they wanted to stay connected. As word spread, additional members began to participate. Eventually, multiple phone meetings were formed that included participants from many parts of the world.

In January 2009, the Board of Trustees (BOT) was asked to discuss the need for additional guidelines for telephone meetings. The process used for these meetings included a member staying on the phone line after the meeting was officially over to talk with newcomers. To make Seventh Tradition donations or contribute to special appeals, individuals were encouraged to send donations directly to the World Service Office (WSO). Telephone meetings continued to grow, and in time, these meetings became more organized and gained acceptance.

History has shown us that meetings come and go. They can grow or stay small for long periods of time. Sometimes they do not survive at all. Technology has provided us with greater opportunities and more meeting choices. Today we can meet face-to-face, on telephone conference calls, via online meetings, and internet video and voice applications.

Attending S-Anon meetings is a fundamental tool for our recovery journey. Meetings provide us with a safe place to share our experiences with others and work together to solve our common problems. It only takes two members to have a meeting. In meetings we learn that we are suffering from a family disease and to focus on our own recovery. We discover the value of working the S-Anon Twelve Steps, Traditions, and Concepts of Service and applying them to our lives. Regular attendance brings members together for healing and personal growth. We are invited to participate in our own time and in our own way.

• • •

Up for Discussion…

1. When and how did I first hear about S-Anon? How long did I wait before attending my first meeting?

2. What were my expectations and actual experiences coming to my first meeting?

3. How willing am I to go some distance to meet with another S-Anon member?

4. Am I willing to start a new meeting if the need arises?

5. Does my group welcome all newcomers and current members equally, in the spirit of Tradition Three?

6. Is my S-Anon group registered with the WSO, so that people seeking help can find support?

7. Have I considered attending or participating in a phone, online, or virtual S-Anon meeting? If yes, what was my experience with this type of meeting.

• • •

S-ANON MEETINGS FOR COUPLES

Many therapists in the 1980s viewed spouses of addicts as co-addicts or codependents, while others did not understand that their clients with compulsive sexual behavior might actually have a sex addiction. They often tried to handle sexual compulsion or acting out behaviors through couples' therapy. Self-help books became prevalent, and many of these books used that terminology. Treating this disease as a "couples' problem" instead of treating each partner's issues separately sometimes led to more distress and fear within the relationship.

> I knew that my husband's affairs had ruined his first marriage, but naively thought this had nothing to do with us as a couple. But two years into the marriage, he told me about an affair — and it wasn't the first since we had been married. We went to a counselor, but back then no one had heard of sex addiction — every problem was attributed to difficulties between the couple.
>
> S-Anon member, questionnaire and personal notes

During this time, both S-Anon and SA were trying to establish themselves as independent fellowships. Attendance at early gatherings was small. It was common practice to have a lot of open meetings where many couples found themselves sitting in the same room. In early 1986, several couples from Oklahoma, Kansas, and Missouri got together for two different couples' weekend retreats. Meetings for couples were also started in their local areas.

National conferences in 1986 and 1987 (these events are now known as international conventions) included sessions on recovery as a couple. An Arizona couple had the idea to organize Twelve Step weekends for couples after attending several of these conferences. The first couples' retreat in Arizona was held in March 1987, and about a dozen couples attended the event. It was held annually for the next seven years. Within a short time, couples' meetings were routinely held at most conferences and regional retreats. They were usually considered a joint meeting and not necessarily associated with either fellowship.

After attending the Arizona retreat, two couples from Los Angeles, California, returned home and started a local couples' meeting. The founder of Sexaholics Anonymous lived in the area and was asked if SA would sanction the meeting. He said they would not. Unaware that an S-Anon Central Office existed where they could have asked for input, the S-Anon members approached their local meeting. The West L.A. S-Anon group agreed to sponsor that couples' meeting.

That meeting was named "S-Anon Committed Couples." It was not intended to replace the regular S-Anon meeting. There was much trial and error in establishing and conducting that couples' meeting. Members of the group created a pamphlet that included a suggested meeting format and readings from both S-Anon and Sexaholics Anonymous. The West Los Angeles S-Anon group approved the pamphlet for use at that couples' meeting.

Prior to the creation of the World Service Conference, decisions for the entire S-Anon fellowship were made at international conferences by those S-Anon members in attendance. At the December 1987 international conference business meeting, the attendees approved a motion to accept "S-Anon Committed Couples" meetings. The pamphlet originally created by the West Los Angeles couples' meeting was also approved.

The following year, the S-Anon Central Office received a letter from the founder of SA that expressed concern about the S-Anon Committed Couples pamphlet. A copy of the pamphlet along with the letter was sent to all registered S-Anon groups with a request that these items be discussed at their next business meetings.

At the January 1989 conference business meeting, the first item on the agenda was the content and layout of the couples' meeting pamphlet. They discussed who would be allowed to attend couples' meetings, if the pamphlet needed SA approval, and what to include in the pamphlet itself. After much discussion, a few edits were made. They decided that S-Anon did not need SA's approval, and the pamphlet was approved.

There was a second issue related to the letter from the founder of SA. He thought the use of the word "committed" implied that the couple might not be married.[2] S-Anon members present at that business meeting voted to change the name to "S-Anon Recovering Couples." The name of the meeting was changed again in 1992 to "S-Anon Couples in Recovery." This was done to avoid confusion with another existing Twelve Step fellowship for couples with a similar name. Today it is most often referred to simply as "S-Anon Couples' Meetings."

From the beginning, couples' meetings have brought up challenging questions and controversy, including the following: How can couples' meetings adhere to the S-Anon Twelve Traditions and other S-Anon spiritual principles? How can sharing at couples' meetings focus on the S-Anon point of view? Do couples have to be married in order to attend? Can one spouse attend without the other? Can a single person attend? Can couples attend if the sex addict is not in recovery or does not stay sober? Can the sex addict attend if they are working a program other than SA for their sex addiction? Should anyone decide for someone else if they can attend a couples' meeting?

All these burning questions and controversies came with many thoughtful discussions and prayerful considerations. The first *S-Anon Group Handbook,* issued in 1993, stated that "Special Meetings," including couples' meetings, were not registered groups. (Registered S-Anon groups are those that agree to abide by all Twelve Traditions of S-Anon and, in particular, agree that their group meetings will be open to all who qualify for S-Anon, in accordance with Tradition Three.)

The S-Anon fellowship has grown in numbers, demographics, and personal recovery. While some members still find S-Anon couples' meetings beneficial, the S-Anon recovery focus has shifted

---

[2] Attendance at S-Anon Couples' Meetings is not restricted to married people. The meetings are open to anyone who wishes to attend.

toward individual recovery. Most international conventions still offer couples' meetings; however, a much broader range of meeting topics that focus on individual S-Anon recovery has developed over the years. Some members choose not to attend couples' meetings, while others continue to find them helpful for their recovery.

Even with declining participation in local S-Anon couples' meetings and recovery events, controversy is still present. Motions have frequently been presented at the annual S-Anon World Service Conference on issues related to these meetings. While fewer S-Anon couples' meetings are available, and they have been designated as open meetings since 2019, they continue to raise questions and challenges.

• • •

Up for Discussion…

1. How can the spiritual principles found in Tradition Three be practiced in couples' meetings?

2. What might be some of the benefits of participating in an S-Anon Couples' meeting with my partner? What might be some drawbacks?

3. How have couples' meetings affected my recovery in S-Anon?

4. How can I practice "Live and Let Live" regarding couples' meetings and other special meetings?

5. Have I ever considered that focusing on my relationship may be an outside issue for my S-Anon recovery? How does this apply to Tradition Ten?

• • •

S-ATEEN

HELP AND HOPE FOR TEENS

> Even if you think you are not affected by problems in your home, many of the choices you make in friendships and dating relationships are influenced by living within a family that is spiritually and emotionally ill. Perhaps you have been affected by someone's sexual behavior outside of your home. The sexaholic in your life may be a family member, classmate, friend, teacher, coach, pastor, or other authority figure.
> From *"Is S-Ateen for You?"*

During our early years, inquiries came up periodically about having recovery groups for teens. A question was printed in the 1990 Spring *S-Anews* asking if there were any programs similar to the Alateen program available for children affected by another person's sex addiction. After discussions at the July 1990 International Conference business meeting, a motion not to develop an S-Ateen program at that time was presented and passed. Members agreed that there were too many other issues that needed our immediate attention. The question was raised again a few years later, and it was suggested that anyone who wished to set up a program could use Alateen guidelines. This directed that each S-Ateen meeting would be guided by two adult S-Anon members serving as S-Ateen Group Sponsors.

> In 1996, an S-Anon member started bringing her sixteen-year-old daughter to the Friday night meeting she attended. For a few weeks the young girl sat in another room, doing her homework while the meeting was in progress. Then one week the group invited her into the meeting. Her mother offered to step out of the room while the daughter shared, and the daughter offered to step out while the mother shared. The members were happy that the teenager could have a safe place to talk.

> At the end of 1996, an S-Anon member stated that her fifteen-year-old son wished there was a group he could go to. He, too, needed a safe and supportive place to deal with the family secrets. That's when another S-Anon member and I began to discuss starting an S-Ateen meeting. After much thought, prayer, and discussion, we became the two adult group sponsors for the first S-Ateen group.
>
> S-Anon member, Warren, Michigan

On Friday, November 1, 1996, the first S-Ateen meeting was held in Clinton Township, Michigan. Three teenagers (a thirteen-year-old girl, a sixteen-year-old girl, and a fifteen-year-old boy) and two adult sponsors were present.

At the January 1998 international convention, an S-Ateen member was a keynote speaker for the first time. A breakout session titled "How to Start an S-Ateen Meeting" was also included in the program. A year later another S-Ateen member spoke at an international convention. Some of that shared experience was printed in *S-Anews*. Here is an excerpt:

> That first S-Anon meeting was a very powerful experience for me. Knowing that it was my first meeting, a woman spoke about her experiences in her family of origin. I knew, given the stuff I had been going through, that I belonged there.
>
> My parents were in the process of a divorce and had been separated for quite some time. One night I received a phone call from my father. He said he had just told his counselor that he had abused me as a child, and the counselor said that it would have to be reported to the authorities. If I had not been in S-Ateen, I probably would not be here today.
>
> Charges were pressed, and my father ended up serving a year in jail. My S-Ateen program helps me realize that I do not need to be ashamed of what happened to me or what I have gone through.
>
> S-Ateen member, *S-Anews,* June 1999

On September 12, 2001, the first S-Ateen meeting in Canada was held in Toronto, Ontario. There were eight sponsors serving on a rotating basis. The S-Ateen meeting met one hour earlier than the local S-Anon meeting. In the beginning, that meeting was financially supported by the local Toronto S-Anon group. Five S-Ateen members regularly attended until most aged out at twenty, and the group closed in 2005.

In July 2004, the first Chairperson of the S-Anon Board of Trustees S-Ateen Committee was approved. The committee renewed efforts to provide S-Ateen meetings at international conventions and to support any member interested in starting a local meeting. A pamphlet titled "S-Ateen-Information about Sponsorship and Meetings" was published in 2006. It was helpful when answering questions about starting new S-Ateen meetings. Although a number of S-Ateen meetings started across the United States and one in Canada, by 2012 there were no known meetings in the United States or Canada.

The BOT position for S-Ateen Committee Chairperson was filled again in 2014 after being vacant since 2008. Meetings for S-Ateen members were usually available at international conventions. In October of 2015, an S-Ateen Online Community website was established. This online community is still offering virtual S-Ateen meetings weekly. In recent years, there has been an S-Ateen track at conventions, with several S-Ateen meetings throughout the weekend. As of this writing, face-to-face S-Ateen meetings take place in Spain, Israel, and the United States.

The S-Ateen Committee developed new guidelines and training material for the group sponsors in 2013. These new documents were approved by the BOT. S-Ateen group sponsor applicants who pass a standard background check are certified through a service training process. S-Ateen group sponsors serve in local and online S-Ateen meetings, as well as at gatherings such as local events or international conventions. Parents of S-Ateen members may serve as group sponsors, but they do not serve at any meetings their child or children attend.

S-Ateen meetings are conducted separately from S-Anon meetings. Two S-Ateen Group Sponsors must be present at every meeting, but the meetings are led by the S-Ateen members. They ask other S-Ateen members or group sponsors to be their individual sponsors. The teens have noted how helpful it has been to be with other young people who are facing similar challenges. Together they can learn to apply the principles of the S-Ateen program as they learn new, healthy ways to live and interact with others. As in S-Anon, the S-Ateen focus is on themselves and their own recovery, not on the sex addict or on other people's problems. Between 2014 and 2020, several pieces of S-Ateen Service Literature have been published, as well as "S-Ateen: What It's Like to Be Me," a Conference Approved Literature booklet written by and for S-Ateen members.

• • •

Up for Discussion…

As an S-Ateen member:

1. In what ways has recovery changed how I relate to others? What is different in recovery about my ability to do schoolwork and carry out my responsibilities at home?

2. Have I joined the S-Ateen Online Community? If so, what have been some of the benefits?

3. Have I visited the section for S-Ateen on the S-Anon website?

4. Am I willing to meet with other S-Ateen members at S-Anon gatherings? Why or why not?

5. What aspects of S-Ateen service work interest me?

6. What does having a sponsor mean to me? What do I look for when considering a sponsor?

7. When I have a sponsor, am I willing to sponsor another S-Ateen member?

8. Do I use the S-Ateen literature as a tool for my recovery?

As an S-Anon member:

1. Have I considered how my children might have been affected by this family disease?

2. How have I handled discussions of the S-Anon or S-Ateen programs with my children?

3. How has my recovery benefited my children? Could my children benefit from reading S-Ateen literature and attending S-Ateen meetings? Am I willing to seek Higher Power's guidance on this idea? Can I talk to my sponsor about it?

4. If I sense that my Higher Power is guiding me to introduce my children to S-Ateen, how might I offer them information?

5. Have I considered becoming an S-Ateen Group Sponsor or starting an S-Ateen meeting?

6. Have I been sharing the principles of recovery with my children in other ways? How?

CHAPTER THREE

S-Anon Recovery Events

Attending regular S-Anon meetings reassured us that we were no longer alone and offered vital support to our recovery. In addition to our local meetings, gathering with other S-Anon members at regional, national, and international gatherings gave us an even greater depth of experience, strength, and hope. These larger events provided us with an increased awareness of the family disease of sex addiction and a broader perspective of our worldwide fellowship. They helped us gain new insights on using the S-Anon Twelve Steps and other program tools to find solutions to our common problems.

Those who attended early S-Anon recovery events greatly helped the fellowship develop and grow. Conferences provided additional opportunities to grow in individual recovery, receive and offer support through sponsorship and service, and hear a wider range of experience than is usually found in local meetings. Members learned that they could participate in service work beyond the group level, and they began to carry the message of recovery through service back to their local groups.

These gatherings served as venues for early discussions about how to create a structure for our fellowship. Members who attended the business meeting during each conference served as our first "service boards," making decisions and voting on motions. The process to establish consistent meeting guidelines and to unify our Conference Approved Literature began at these conferences.

• • •

THE STRUGGLE OF FINDING OUR S-ANON VOICE

The first known gathering of S-Anon members outside of local meetings took place at the Sexaholics Anonymous Conference in Simi Valley, California, in December 1983. This was the beginning of a long journey to form our own identity while cooperating with recovering sex addicts to host events. Until 2004, large events were referred to by several names, including national conferences and international conventions. Beginning in 2004, these semi-annual events became known as international conventions. Regional conventions and one-day recovery events also continued to be held.

From the beginning, S-Anon members desired to have a voice in planning these conferences. Conflicts arose at the December 1983 event because SA had planned the S-Anon portion of the weekend. A consensus was reached within S-Anon to plan our own program at future conferences. This was a turning point for our fellowship in having a voice and defining our own S-Anon identity. One of the S-Anon women offered to represent S-Anon at the planning sessions of the next SA conference.

In June 1984, the fourth Sexaholics Anonymous National Conference took place in Salt Lake City, Utah. Twelve to fourteen S-Anon members attended. There is no specific S-Anon program information available, but sessions were mostly combined meetings with SA. Since then, S-Anon members have served on the planning committees for conventions and other events held in cooperation with SA.

The fifth SA National Conference was held in Phoenix, Arizona, in December 1984. The SA keynote speaker was an expert in the field of sex addiction. This was significant to S-Anon members in attendance, as this doctor was one of only a few professionals at that time speaking about help for the suffering family member. This was the first time SA decided to have an outside speaker, rather than a member of the SA fellowship, address the conference attendees.

Once again, the meetings available for S-Anon members at this conference were mostly combined with SA. Spouses and other family members of the addicts expressed gratitude for being included in their meetings, but also began to realize that these combined meetings were not as helpful for their recovery as they had hoped. Some S-Anon members spoke up and expressed discomfort at attending what were called "joint sessions."

Hearing so much sharing from the sex addicts' perspective often brought up emotional pain and anger for many S-Anon members. They wanted to hear S-Anon members share their experiences.

They needed to learn how to apply their own tools of recovery. Many members did not feel safe sharing their own experiences while attending joint sessions. As a result, additional S-Anon-only meetings were gradually added to conference programs.

We began using our voice to plan our own events. The Northwest Regional SA Conference took place in June 1985 in Warm Beach, Washington. Eight S-Anon members attended. The weekend activities included five S-Anon closed sessions, some combined meetings, and open speaker meetings. Later that year, the first one-day SA and S-Anon recovery event was held in the Baltimore/Washington, D.C. area.

During the next few years there was slow but steady progress in strengthening our resolve to have our own identity at these cooperative recovery events. In April 1986, the "First All-Day Conference of the Eastern Region of SA and S-Anon" was held in New York City, New York. This regional event included three closed S-Anon breakout sessions, as well as the combined opening and closing sessions. The program title acknowledged the event as both SA and S-Anon.

The first nationwide S-Anon gathering in Germany took place in the spring of 1986. About 20 women spent the weekend in a retreat facility. The accommodations were modest, and they cooked their own meals. Five years later, S-Anon members in Germany began holding recovery events in cooperation with SA once a year, while still maintaining an annual S-Anon-only gathering.

In June 1986, the SA National Conference took place in Kansas City, Missouri. The printed program displayed both the SA and S-Anon logos and included a few separate sessions just for S-Anon. Eight S-Anon members attended the event.

Twenty S-Anon members attended the SA National Conference held in St. Louis, Missouri, in December 1986. There were six S-Anon closed breakout sessions and five combined or open sessions. The open sessions were speaker panels, all of which included one S-Anon member. There was an open "Recovery Workshop" that dealt with issues for married couples, single members, married members with a spouse not in recovery, and those who did not identify as heterosexual. This marked another shift in thinking about our own needs.

Sometimes there were confusing messages when it came to a gathering of S-Anon and SA members. The title for the June 1987 Bozeman, Montana Conference was "Semi-Annual International SA Conference." Although S-Anon participated and the S-Anon logo appeared, the title mentioned only SA. The printed program identified one S-Anon session per time slot. We know an S-Anon business meeting took place, but it was not identified on the program.

> S-Anon sharing at conferences was more helpful to me personally than I could ever have imagined. The first conference I attended was particularly memorable. Surrounded by caring S-Anon members who understood, I finally felt safe enough to feel my pain.
>
> My grief had built up over 25 years, three marriages, and other dysfunctional relationships, and it was time for me to heal. I was able to admit to myself that some of my actions had caused people I care about, including myself, heartache and trouble. I cried for a hefty portion of two days straight. The relief was indescribable! These were healing tears, not tears of rage and frustration.
>
> The tendency toward isolation and feeling "apart from" that seems to be a large part of my disease was replaced with a wonderful feeling of being a "part of." As I heard people share their stories, I saw myself. Some of my old ideas were finally exposed as the rationalizations they were. Pride made me cling to these thoughts, and they kept me locked into the pain that was so hurtful and yet so familiar.
>
> I could see that I needed to be free of that form of denial, or further healing would not be possible. I thought I had already taken the First Step, but it was during that conference that I felt my powerlessness at the gut level. I'm so grateful to my Higher Power for that experience, for all of you out there, and for this program of recovery.
>
> S-Anon member, *S-Anews*, Summer 1989

• • •

Up for Discussion…

1. Have I attended a regional or international gathering of S-Anon? Why or why not?

2. What was my experience when attending a recovery event? How do I practice self-care at recovery events?

3. What impact has gathering with other S-Anon members had on my life? How do I experience my Higher Power at recovery events?

4. How has a wider circle, usually found at larger events, strengthened my own recovery?

5. How has hearing the experiences of S-Anon members at these larger events changed the way I understand my part in the family disease?

• • •

ESTABLISHING OUR S-ANON IDENTITY

S-Anon demonstrated our clear and separate purpose at the December 1987 conference in Los Angeles, California. This conference was identified as "Semi-annual International SA Convention and S-Anon Convention." A program schedule for each fellowship was printed on separate pages instead of combined.

For the first time, S-Anon offered two breakout sessions per time slot. Other differences included two specific sessions for couples and only one open speaker meeting. A separate business meeting and its location were identified on the program. The shared luncheon was hosted by S-Anon and was followed by an S-Anon recovery birthday celebration.

As S-Anon attendance grew at the semi-annual conventions, many members encountered scheduling difficulties, so convention dates were moved from December and June to January and July. To accommodate this transition, only one international convention took place in 1988, in July in Rochester, New York. Program schedules continued to be printed separately. S-Anon hosted the Saturday luncheon that included two S-Anon speakers. The schedule also allotted time for an S-Anon business meeting.

Before this event, the S-Anon Central Office received a letter from the local Rochester S-Anon planning committee requesting clarification about combined events. The National SA Conference Committee had wanted to know if the S-Anon Central Office had concerns with any of the scheduled joint sessions or the combined birthday celebrations. This was another indication that S-Anon was gaining an independent identity.

> The first few conventions I attended had 20–30 S-Anon members. I remember that I heard S-Anon members talk about being grateful. I couldn't understand how they could be "grateful members of S-Anon." I was also blown away by the honesty and ability to talk clearly about something that had been such a guarded secret my entire life.
>
> Conventions were difficult for me to attend because of the expense. I went to the Detroit convention by a 24-hour bus ride. I did that while my husband wasn't in recovery. I also went to Philadelphia without him. I went with another S-Anon member.
>
> S-Anon member from Georgia
>
> A combined S-Anon and SA Regional Southern California Unity Conference was first held in 1989. The Los Angeles area had a few S-Anon meetings that were spread out over a large region. There were also some lone members, those who didn't have access to a local meeting. Having a regional conference was a way to get to know each other and bring unity to many S-Anon members. Interest in this event grew, and the second conference had 75 S-Anon members in attendance. This annual event continues to attract members from many different locations.

By 1989, S-Anon conferences took place in Germany twice a year and lasted four days. There were male S-Anon members attending some of these early conferences. Sometimes dogs and kids were also present.

Due to better accommodations, we were free to organize evenings of music and entertainment such as dance, sketches, reading fairy tales, singing, and drumming. These evenings were very emotional and involved both laughter and crying. Usually, these conferences had 25 to 40 S-Anon members in attendance.

S-Anon history file

• • •

Up for Discussion…

1. Have my local groups considered hosting an S-Anon-only event? Why or why not? Are we willing to consider it?

2. Have I participated in planning or hosting an S-Anon recovery event? If so, what was my experience?

3. How do I practice the spiritual principles of the S-Anon Twelve Traditions and Twelve Concepts of Service when planning a cooperative event with recovering sex addicts? Which recovery tools might be helpful?

• • •

SHAPING OUR S-ANON IDENTITY

Some S-Anon members attended conferences or conventions simply because their spouses were going to the SA event. Others went hoping to enrich their individual recovery or to find a sponsor. As the fellowship grew, these events became a place for making business decisions and approving literature. S-Anon's identity continued to take shape as the fellowship became more independent, and we made more decisions for ourselves, with a Higher Power guiding our group conscience.

Some areas began to host S-Anon-only independent activities. In October 1991, an S-Anon retreat was held in the Chicago, Illinois area. Nineteen people attended that weekend. This retreat became an annual event that still meets as of this publication.

> I have been home from the 1992 Chicago Area S-Anon retreat for six hours now. The retreat was one of the most enjoyable, hard, fun, painful, and exhaustive experiences I have undertaken in my almost two years of recovery. I didn't know what to expect. I had gone to a one-day workshop for another Twelve Step program, but this was a whole weekend. Overnight. Two nights!
>
> There were 38 S-Anon members ready to "Peel the Onion," which was the theme of the retreat. A wide variety of topics were offered, from "Grieving" to "Rebuilding our Sexual Selves." We were privileged to hear two members share their Step One experience. There was time for fellowship, walks in the woods, and meditation. On Sunday evening after the retreat was over, nine of us gathered in the lounge to talk about our childhoods and the family pets we had owned.
>
> I am grateful to everyone on the committee and those who attended the retreat for making it possible for me to have this experience.
>
> S-Anon member, *S-Anews*, Winter 1992–1993

Speakers and various breakout sessions are often recorded at S-Anon international conventions. Initially, S-Anon sold copies of these recordings as a source of revenue. Currently, either S-Anon or a private company handles recording and sales. Some of these early recordings were also transcribed and used in *S-Anews* or Conference Approved Literature. This was a way for our fellowship to share the message of our recovery.

One of the continuing challenges with recorded sessions has been the concern about anonymity when voices might be recognized.

Recorded breakout sessions were, and still are, clearly identified in the printed program, so that members who do not wish their sharing to be recorded could choose to attend other sessions. Some members raised questions about having too many recorded sessions. Host groups responded by making efforts to include more meetings that were not recorded.

Another challenge occurred when Traditions were not adhered to during sharing in a recorded meeting. Members sometimes expressed a concern to the meeting leader, the convention team, or a member of the Board of Trustees (BOT). After careful review, the convention team or BOT occasionally determined that a recording would not be made available for sale.

This important practice continues today. Members who are unable to attend gatherings or who have difficulty finding local meetings may find recordings from S-Anon events helpful in their recovery.

To host an S-Anon international convention, local volunteers coordinate with the S-Anon International Convention Committee (ICC). Over the years S-Anon has established guidelines for planning these activities, including selecting the location and venue, planning the program, cooperating with SA, and handling finances. S-Anon groups and intergroups also plan retreats, one-day recovery events, and regional events.

S-Anon members have participated in recovery events since the 1980s. These gatherings have also been held in many other countries. S-Anon international conventions are now only held in the United States and Canada. Other countries may hold their own conventions, although members from all over the world are welcome to attend S-Anon international conventions.[3]

For many years, S-Anon members had to either mail their conference or convention registration to the WSO or go to the SA

---

[3]The July 2017 S-Anon/S-Ateen and SA International Conventions were held in Israel. Many S-Anon and S-Ateen members attended that convention, but after the experience of a holding a convention outside the United States and Canada, S-Anon determined that we do not have sufficient resources for our WSO to support future international conventions in other countries.

website to register online. As S-Anon attendance grew at these international events, and our understanding of the Twelve Traditions increased, so did the desire to have a separate registration system. Creating this system was a sizable undertaking. In November 2013, the Board of Trustees (BOT) approved the purchase of software that would allow registration for S-Anon and S-Ateen members via the S-Anon website. This new system was activated in the fall of 2014.

In 2017, the SA fellowship chose to accept a bid to hold its January 2019 international convention in Europe. In July 2017, the ICC Chairperson brought a motion to the BOT to hold the first S-Anon-only international convention in January 2019. The motion was unanimously approved. This decision was in recognition of the fact that S-Anon and SA are two separate and distinct fellowships. We decided to plan our own international convention in Nashville, Tennessee.

The planning committee for this event included the World Service Office (WSO) staff, several members of the Executive Committee, and members of the ICC. The Tennessee Intergroup and numerous other volunteers also assisted with the planning process.

This historic event took place in January 2019. Attendance included 7 S-Ateen members, 3 WSO staff members, and 184 S-Anon members. The program included more than 40 S-Anon breakout sessions, 6 S-Ateen sessions, 2 speaker meetings, a birthday celebration, and a closing gratitude meeting. There were 90 volunteers who provided support in planning and implementing this event. The past 35 years of finding our voice, considering our needs, and planning our gatherings culminated in what most attendees described as a very successful, meaningful, and spiritually uplifting experience.

The lengthy process of finding our voice has been multi-faceted. These larger gatherings have helped S-Anon to identify and clearly express our needs. We gained independence from the SA program and learned what "cooperating" in a recovery event means to our fellowship. We learned the importance of respecting the Traditions when sharing at meetings, speaking at gatherings, and protecting the recording and sales of S-Anon voices.

When S-Anon members come together to share their experience, strength, and hope, great things happen, not only for individuals, but for the hosting groups and S-Anon as a whole. Members develop friendships, find sponsors and sponsees, experience spiritual awakenings, and volunteer for opportunities to serve our fellowship. After attending these events, members pass on the message of S-Anon recovery. Many members have expressed that these gatherings have aided their recovery and given them hope for healing and a better way of life.

• • •

Up for Discussion…

1. How am I learning to use my voice as I recover in S-Anon?

2. Have I considered volunteering for service if I plan to attend a recovery event? Why or why not?

3. Do I see how the Twelve Traditions and Twelve Concepts of Service are observed (or not observed) at an S-Anon gathering? What would my options and responsibilities be if they are not observed?

4. When speaking or sharing in meetings, do I consider our common welfare as expressed in Tradition One and whether I'm speaking from the S-Anon point of view?

5. Have I acknowledged or sought a Higher Power's guidance when participating in a group conscience decision?

6. Am I open to change? How do I experience following guidelines and suggestions?

CHAPTER FOUR

Literature: Unifying the S-Anon Message

OUT WITH THE OLD, IN WITH THE NEW

This chapter describes the monumental task necessary to create and publish S-Anon Conference Approved Literature and highlights the importance of having literature written from the S-Anon point of view.

When members attended an S-Anon meeting in the 1980s, they would have been warmly greeted and probably handed sheets of paper with various readings. Those readings differed from meeting to meeting. Many of them did not specifically address the S-Anon problem.

Some of the readings were from other Twelve Step programs or gave tips from counseling professionals. There may have been a page with a list of recommended books to read. The collection of handouts included the following titles: *The Dilemma, Do's and Don'ts, Helping, What is Co-Dependency?, The Three Deadly Enemies, Explanation of Compulsive Lusting, Let It Begin with Me, Help Yourself Now,* and *Definition of an S-Anon Member*. These readings are no longer available, as they were not written from the S-Anon point of view. They were temporarily used before we had our own S-Anon CAL.

Since our first gathering in 1983, members have discussed the need for S-Anon printed material. Two early members agreed to co-author a pamphlet titled *The Co-Addict's Check List*. It was written from the S-Anon perspective and was available the following spring. Some members were fortunate to have had access to it, but others did not. Due to distance and lack of communication, not everyone knew about the pamphlet or other resources.

Growing out of a strong desire to connect through our own literature, members of the West Los Angeles, California group began the long process of writing about each of the Twelve Steps from the S-Anon point of view. They finished their project in mid-1987. This document was then photocopied, placed into a folder, and made available to our members from the Central Office in Sherman Oaks, California.

> In 1987 the *S-Anon Twelve Step Study* was originally written for the West Los Angeles group. We had previously requested permission to use Al-Anon Conference Approved Literature and adapt it to the S-Anon problem. Al-Anon would not give us permission, but wisely suggested we needed to write our own interpretation.
>
> A handful of people contributed to this writing, using Alcoholics Anonymous and Al-Anon literature as a guide. We met before the Saturday night meeting every week for almost a year sharing on the contents for the Steps.
>
> This was the beginning of creating S-Anon literature from our own experience. Once more, here was God's mysterious way: people who were gifted in writing and editing attended those sessions.
> S-Anon member, West Los Angeles, California, questionnaire

Much of that document was eventually incorporated into our first published book, *S-Anon Twelve Steps*.

Business meetings usually took place at national conferences. A larger representation of members led to more thoughtful and meaningful group conscience discussions and decisions. Voting to approve literature was part of these face-to-face meetings. This was the beginning of S-Anon's process for Conference Approved Literature. To have adequate recovery material available, members agreed that CAL would also include literature from Alcoholic Anonymous (AA), Al-Anon, and Sexaholics Anonymous.

The business meeting at the December 1987 conference included a discussion of unified literature. Attendees agreed that the literature needed to be consolidated and consistent across all groups throughout the United States. The *S-Anon Twelve Step Study*, written and used by the West Los Angeles group, was introduced at that conference, and a motion was made to consider it for CAL. The motion did not pass because those who were present expressed a need to have sufficient time for members to use it in their meetings and give feedback before final approval.

The attendees decided to vote again at the next conference, or later, if more time was needed. Groups were reminded that the *S-Anon Twelve Step Study* was not yet CAL and that we were still working on the copyright status. They were told that we could not sell this literature, but donations would be accepted.

• • •

COMMITMENT TO OUR OWN LITERATURE

Creating a consistent message through S-Anon literature helped unite our fellowship in a common cause. Members who attended the conference business meetings often voiced the need for our own literature. As efforts to create and approve our own literature continued, interest in S-Anon was growing.

Before S-Anon had much literature available, the Central Office sent out newcomer packets that included some material that was not Conference Approved Literature. The newcomer packet was primarily a collection of readings that were not our own. Members often took outside readings and retyped them by replacing words to better fit the S-Anon program. This rewording was often different from group to group. These changes were made without seeking permission from the original source. The Central Office used one version of those readings to send to inquirers in the newcomer packet.

Many groups were still unclear as to why using outside literature during meetings was not in our best interest. At that time, most members did not have an understanding of the Twelve Traditions. People were eager to find help, so some groups chose to continue using outside literature. This was one indication of just how essential it was to have writing from the S-Anon point of view that would focus on our own problem and solution and eliminate the need for outside literature.

S-Anon members lacked experience in how to create and approve literature as a unified fellowship. Not only was the fellowship new, but the members lacked the depth of understanding to express the spiritual principles of the S-Anon program. Most members did not realize how much concentrated work it would take to create our own literature.

The creation of the S-Anon International Committee (SIC) was approved at the conference business meeting in January 1989. Overseeing S-Anon literature was part of the SIC's responsibilities. Their literature duties included keeping track of what had been Conference Approved, as well as writing new literature.

Several pieces of literature were presented for consideration during the business meeting at that conference. The *S-Anon Twelve Step Study* was approved as CAL, pending permission from AA and Al-Anon to use quotes from their publications. Members also decided that an SA writing was unsuitable for our newcomer packet and voted to remove it. The SIC also agreed to rewrite other pieces for that packet.

Modifications to the *Suggested Meeting Format* were approved and incorporated into all related documents. The *Meeting Format* provided consistent guidance and language for conducting a meeting and was printed in several pamphlets and in the *Leader's Manual*. The SIC also made a few minor edits to a brochure for couples' meetings with the understanding that additional changes would be forthcoming.

The SIC soon found themselves spending numerous hours dealing with literature. This work was done prior to widespread use of the Internet and other electronic communication technologies, making what was already a lengthy process even slower. The primary sources of communication during this time included costly long-distance telephone calls, postal mail, and fax. The amount of care, time, and work needed to produce literature was a challenge for the SIC.

Some literature-related motions were passed at the July 1989 conference business meeting. They reflected efforts by the SIC to address the issue of outside literature during meetings as well as to clarify and expand the *Leader's Manual*. The updated *Leader's Manual* included a meeting format, guidelines for a meeting, the S-Anon Twelve Steps, S-Anon Twelve Traditions, and various CAL readings that could be used in a meeting. This revision included removing, replacing, or modifying several of the readings already in use.

Letters were frequently sent out to groups informing them about SIC decisions and various motions passed at these conference business meetings. Communications often included requests for help with writing and other literature needs. Part of one such letter, dated October 27, 1989, stated the following:

> We are writing to you at this time to request your help. Part of the responsibility of the S-Anon International Committee is to address the urgent need for our own Conference Approved Literature. One way we do this is by putting a "call out for writing"' to all S-Anon members to do the writing themselves, then through following the channels, getting it ready for publication…

This letter also outlined the process for Conference Approval. It included an announcement about a new service position called "Reader." Once a writing was submitted and reviewed by the SIC, the Readers would be asked to review it, answer a questionnaire, correct typos, and offer suggested changes. The desired goal was to have six or seven Readers from across the United States to provide a broader perspective to the "voice" of S-Anon.

We needed permission from both AA and Al-Anon to use quotes from their literature for the completed *S-Anon Twelve Step Study*, which had been Conference Approved at the conference business meeting in January 1989. Both of those permissions were received by January 1990. After years of development, the *S-Anon Twelve Step Study* booklet was finally ready for publication and sale. Our Central Office secretary assembled our first CAL booklet. She copied and punched holes in the pages and placed them in colorful labeled folders. It took ten years from that point to publish the *S-Anon Twelve Steps* book we use today.

We are grateful for the willingness and perseverance of those S-Anon members who write and edit the literature we use. We have seen a Higher Power guide them through the completion of all our literature projects.

• • •

Up for Discussion…

1. What literature was present at my first meeting? How was it helpful to me?

2. Why is it important that S-Anon literature be unified?

3. When a piece of literature takes a long time to be completed, do I trust my Higher Power's timing, or do I become frustrated and try to force solutions?

4. How are newcomers to my group introduced to S-Anon CAL? Does my group provide them with a copy of the newcomer's booklet, *We're Glad You're Here*?

5. How does CAL continue to help me in my recovery?

• • •

FORMATION OF THE LITERATURE COMMITTEE

Throughout 1989 and 1990, it was the responsibility of the SIC to review the literature we were using. After thoughtful discussion and consideration, they agreed on what literature to approve. 1990 was a productive year for completing literature projects. Many projects were started and most came to fruition, as members used their written voices to carry the message of recovery from the effects of another's sex addiction.

Efforts to update the newcomer packet continued. Several readings were removed, and others were revised. Several new writings were submitted with the goal of creating a pamphlet that would eventually replace the newcomer packet. Two other new pamphlets were completed. One was titled *Sexaholism: A Family Disease* and the other was geared toward couples' issues. "Obstacles to Recovery," a reading that originated from Al-Anon, was adapted for our use.

After permission from Al-Anon was received, this became one of our CAL readings used in meetings.

The SIC spent a lot of time talking about literature and considered forming a separate committee to focus on our literature. They discussed how this committee would function to allow the SIC to spend more time on other business matters. The formation of a Literature Committee (LC) was approved at the January 1991 conference business meeting. It would be responsible to the fellowship as a whole, but would participate with and report to the SIC. A letter was sent to the fellowship in March 1991 explaining this change:

> Having a Literature Committee is a big step for S-Anon. Current members of the SIC have spent a good portion of time during their terms of service working on literature concerns. These issues often take up much of the discussion time on the SIC monthly conference calls.
>
> Creating a separate committee and having separate conference calls would allow more energy to be focused on producing literature. It would bring in more volunteers and allow for a fuller discussion of issues. Our literature carries the S-Anon message both within our program and to those who have never heard of S-Anon or sex addiction. We feel it needs more time and attention than the SIC is able to devote to it.

A member volunteered to be the first Chairperson of the LC. This Chairperson would also serve as a member of the SIC. As the committee was being formed, members at the group level expressed a strong desire and commitment to work on presenting a unified message in our literature. By becoming involved, they were using their voices in S-Anon's decision-making process.

A letter was received in the spring of 1991 from a group in Michigan about two literature issues. They submitted two motions for consideration and a vote at the next conference business meeting. Their first motion was to revise all references to the sexaholic within the "Meeting Format." The rationale given was that the existing wording in "The S-Anon Welcome" assumed that all members were currently living with sexaholics, which was not necessarily the case. They included a list of specific wording and suggested changes.

Their second motion concerned the use of a Sexaholics Anonymous writing titled *What is a Sexaholic and What is Sexual Sobriety?* This reading was found in our *Leader's Manual* and newcomer packet. Since its initial approval, questions had been frequently raised regarding this document. It was then proposed to remove it altogether. The rationale was stated as follows: "Our purpose in sharing is to discuss ourselves, NOT the sexaholic."

The SIC discussed both motions at the July 1991 Conference Business Meeting and agreed that decisions on these issues could be made by the SIC and the LC. They voted unanimously to accept the suggested changes to the "Meeting Format," and to remove the SA reading from our *Leader's Manual* and newcomer packet. While some members felt that the reading served as a valuable reminder of the disease concept of sexaholism, most felt that it did tend to shift our focus to the sexaholic and had caused problems in some groups.

• • •

THE LITERATURE COMMITTEE GETS TO WORK

During 1991, several volunteers stepped forward to join the LC. They had a huge task before them. Initial goals were to get the *S-Anon Twelve Steps* printed in spiral-bound form, add Step stories, and collect writings for the *S-Anon Twelve Traditions*. Other plans included reviewing the literature that was currently in use to decide if it was relevant as CAL or needed to be updated. Discussions took place to identify literature needs. New guidelines for writing, reviewing, and approving CAL were developed. It was decided to have two series of pamphlets: the *Stepping Stones Toward Recovery* series and the *Recovery in Action* series.

The LC Editors had been meeting via telephone conference calls and discussed the benefits of having an extended face-to-face meeting. They chose to come together at the Central Office in California. This first in-person meeting was held in January 1992, three days prior to the international convention in San Diego.

The primary goal was to complete partially written literature so that it could be considered for a vote and approval at the upcoming convention.

> Three Literature Committee members stayed in my home for three days and two nights just before the January 1992 Convention. We did a tremendous amount of work in just a few days. Some of our current literature was reviewed, evaluated, and edited. Written contributions from members were considered, edited, and incorporated. We also wrote new material.
>
> Seven pieces of literature were completed and presented for Conference Approval. As so often happens while doing service work, we also had a good time getting to know each other.
>
> LC member, Southern California

Those seven pieces of newly completed literature were displayed on boards for S-Anon members at the convention to read and consider. At the scheduled business meeting later that weekend, all seven pieces of literature were unanimously approved.

Five of the approved pieces became known as the *Stepping Stones Toward Recovery* series. The individual booklets are no longer in print. Some of the material from these booklets was later incorporated into our published book, *Working the S-Anon Program.* The titles of the *Stepping Stones Towards Recovery* series booklets were as follows:

1. *What is a "Slip" and How Do We Stay Sober In S-Anon?*

2. *How Can I Learn to Focus on Myself, Not My Partner?*

3. *How do Periods of Abstinence Affect S-Anon Members?*

4. *How Can I Explain S-Anon to My Children and Begin to Make Amends?*

5. *How Much Should I Tell My Friends and Family About S-Anon?*

> The *Stepping Stones Toward Recovery* series of booklets contains sharing by members on questions that may arise during our recovery in S-Anon. Even though our individual experiences may have been different, we discovered that other members of S-Anon shared similar feelings. So it is in recovery. We approach these questions in our own way, but other S-Anon members surely know how it feels to honestly explore these issues. By becoming more aware of the paths that others have traveled, we learn that we are not alone in our search, even though we each ultimately find our own answers.
>
> Cover of a *Stepping Stones Toward Recovery* series booklet

A member from the LC submitted a brief article in the Spring 1992 *S-Anews*:

> Thanks to all those who read the literature, came to the business meeting, and unanimously supported its approval. Reading the outpouring of experience, strength, and hope in the new literature and hearing the comments of others who read it was truly moving. I can't tell you how much it thrills me that we doubled the amount of our literature.

• • •

WRITING FROM OUR MEMBERS

Another motion approved at the January 1992 conference was to change the definition of "Conference Approved" literature. After the SIC reviewed and approved the final version of a literature draft, the Readers would "act for the members of S-Anon." They voted whether to approve or not approve the literature by postal mail ballot. This would eliminate waiting for the next conference business meeting to obtain final CAL votes.

In late 1992, the SIC sent a letter to the fellowship clarifying the changes made in the literature approval process. Throughout that year, work continued on the *S-Anon Newcomers Booklet*. This new booklet received final approval in January 1993 and was published shortly thereafter. The title of this piece has since been changed to *We're Glad You're Here...Helpful Information for the Newcomer*, though it is frequently referred to simply as the *Newcomers Booklet*.

The booklet Recovering *Together: Issues Faced by Couples in Recovery* was published in 1993. It was revised in 2007 and the title was changed to *Recovering Together: Issues Faced by Couples*. This booklet is available as CAL.

Numerous questions related to our Traditions had been directed to the SIC. The LC decided to address those issues by creating the *Group Handbook*. This was the result of a growing need for guidelines on how to apply the Twelve Traditions. It also contained a summary of the service structure and how the group conscience functions at the group, regional, and fellowship levels.

The *Group Handbook* was updated and improved several times throughout the years. After S-Anon transitioned to the Board of Trustees service structure, major modifications were needed. The *Group Handbook* was renamed the *S-Anon/S-Ateen Service Manual* (SSSM) and published in 2007. A much-needed update to the *SSSM* began in 2015. Revisions were submitted to the BOT, but none of them were approved. In 2017, an ad-hoc committee was established to revise the *SSSM*. The *SSSM* is now stored and available in the member section of the S-Anon website, *member.sanon.org,* making it more convenient for future updates and for members to access the most recent edition.

Since the early years of S-Anon, members have discussed having a combined S-Anon Twelve Steps and Twelve Traditions book. The LC attempted to work on this project several times, but financial challenges in the early 1990s sent priorities in a different direction. In January 1994, the LC agreed that expanding the *S-Anon Twelve Step Study* should be their next focus. Their vision was to include additional material, member stories, and questions for working the Steps. They hoped this would lay the groundwork for a future combined S-Anon Twelve Steps and Twelve Traditions book.

One ongoing obstacle the LC faced was obtaining new writing submissions from the fellowship. Frequent appeals were made through *S-Anews,* and letters were sent to all known groups. (*S-Anews* was a quarterly publication supported by member subscriptions and the last issue was published in 2012.) Sometimes writing sessions were set up at International Conventions. After adequate submissions were received, the time-consuming effort to edit and publish literature began. This labor of love was, and still is, done by unpaid volunteers, except for our professional formatters, who prepare CAL material for publication.

The following letter sent to the fellowship in April 1994 is an example of one appeal for writing from our members:

> The next major project that the Literature Committee will be working on is the creation of an S-Anon Twelve and Twelve. This is a big project, and your help is wanted and needed. Two years ago, several groups taped Steps and Traditions discussions and sent them in to be transcribed. We are in need of more people who have the time and skill to transcribe these tapes. We are also still in need of personal stories for Steps Seven, Eight, and Nine, and Traditions Four through Twelve.

The LC continued working on the expanded *S-Anon Twelve Step Study* through 1999. As a result of determination and commitment, slow but steady progress was made. Sections were rewritten and the Step stories were updated. A new section called "Practicing These Principles" was added to each Step. This section provided additional context to help us overcome any challenges we might have in embracing the Steps. Questions to guide us in applying and working through each of the Steps were also added. The cover was designed, and the book was formatted by volunteers who had the necessary skills. Then it was professionally printed and bound. *S-Anon Twelve Steps* debuted and was available for purchase at the January 2000 international convention in Nashville, Tennessee. There were approximately 2,500 copies sold in the first year.

In mid-1999, as the final stage of this project was nearing completion, the LC started collecting stories for a Twelve Traditions book. This would complete the second half of the planned S-Anon Twelve Steps and Twelve Traditions book. The LC attempted to work on the project, but they lacked adequate submissions and volunteers to produce it at that time.

While the Twelve Traditions project was on hold, the LC was working on another major project. Our fellowship was invited to submit writings on various recovery topics. These writings were eventually incorporated into our daily reader, *Reflections of Hope,* which was published in 2008. Further information on *Reflections of Hope* will be included in Chapter Five of this book.

In 2012, the LC began a concerted effort to write and edit the *S-Anon Twelve Traditions* book. Since that time, a tremendous amount of writing and editing has taken place. In order to make this vital literature available to our members as soon as reasonably possible, the WSO began to publish booklets containing three Tradition chapters as they became CAL. A booklet titled *S-Anon Traditions One, Two, and Three* was published in 2017. It was followed by *S-Anon Traditions Four, Five, and Six* in 2018. *S-Anon Traditions Seven, Eight, and Nine* was published in 2020, and *S-Anon Traditions Ten, Eleven, and Twelve,* in 2021. The initial vision of publishing a combined S-Anon Twelve Steps and Twelve Traditions book became two separate books, one on the Steps and the other on the Traditions. This allows for more publication flexibility. The introduction to the Traditions was approved as CAL, and the book, *S-Anon Twelve Traditions,* was published in 2022.

Literature written from the S-Anon point of view can be helpful to anyone recovering from the effects of sex addiction. It offers experience, strength, and hope as we seek our own individual recovery. Through the guidance of a Higher Power, early S-Anon members understood the benefit of having our own literature. It is an example of how "giving it away" can help us keep what we have been given. We are grateful for their initiative, commitment, and willingness to participate in this valuable service.

• • •

Up for Discussion…

1. What are some differences between S-Anon Conference Approved Literature and outside literature?

2. Does my group lend non-CAL or use it for discussion during our meetings? Am I willing to remind my group of the principles found in the Twelve Traditions when someone suggests we use literature that is not S-Anon CAL? Why or why not?

3. Am I aware that a detailed process for developing CAL is described in our *S-Anon/S-Ateen Service Manual*? Am I willing to learn about it? How does the CAL process reflect recovery principles?

4. Do I understand that all CAL published by S-Anon is written only by S-Anon members? How does this affect my perception of the importance of having literature written from the S-Anon point of view?

5. How does Tradition Six apply to non-CAL?

6. Have I considered submitting writing or serving as a Reader on the LC? Am I willing to talk to my sponsor or other S-Anon member about it?

CHAPTER FIVE

Literature from the S-Anon Point of View

Sharing our recovery experiences in written form has brought help and hope to many people. Writing honestly about our own attitudes and behaviors can be rewarding and healing. We are grateful to those individuals who have shared their S-Anon recovery stories. The amount of S-Anon Conference Approved Literature (CAL) has increased considerably because of their courage.

Listening to and reading about the experiences of other members helps with the process of healing in many ways. Members are relieved to learn they are not alone. Sharing during meetings may be the first time they speak about how their lives have been affected by sexaholism. Some members are ready to talk and speak up right away. Others find their stories too painful to share and take longer to use their voices during meetings. Eventually sharing becomes a way to give back what they have received.

The same is true when writing S-Anon CAL. Our recovery experiences are diverse. As we continue to write literature, more members are able to identify with the problem and find hope.

Working the S-Anon Program

In February 2000, the LC decided to combine some of the CAL pamphlets and booklets into a book. The idea for this new book came about after they began working on a new CAL booklet on the tools of recovery. The new book would include parts of the *Stepping Stones Toward Recovery* series and the *Recovery in Action* series. There was also a draft of a booklet called the *Tools of Recovery*. Since there was good information in this draft piece, and an extensive amount of work was done on it by the Editors over a long period of time, its content would also be included in the new book. A brief description of the S-Anon Twelve Steps and Twelve Traditions would be added, along with stories from members on various topics.

The initial version of the Traditions section was printed in the March 2001 *S-Anews*. The Literature Committee asked for feedback as well as additional stories of how members used the Traditions within their S-Anon groups or their personal lives. By the end of that year, the book was essentially complete. Financial constraints delayed the publication until January 2003. *Working the S-Anon Program* has become a valuable resource for many members.

> Each member uses the tools that work best for him or her. We have even found that some things that did not work for us in early recovery become mainstays later. We use what helps us today and leave the rest for later.
>
> *Working the S-Anon Program*, 2nd ed., p. 2

In July 2008, two concerns were raised regarding the book. One was that it often used the term "spouse" which left out others affected by sexaholism such as children, parents, friends, and coworkers of sex addicts, as well as single people. The second was that the Traditions might have been violated by including sharing from members of an outside program.

The LC had already planned to review the book before a second printing. They used this opportunity to review it more carefully and make revisions to address these concerns. An index, the S-Anon Twelve Concepts of Service, and more member stories were also included. Making these changes and taking the revised piece through the CAL process was more difficult and involved than they anticipated.

The World Service Office (WSO) sold out of First Edition copies while waiting for revisions to be completed. Orders for the books could not be filled for seven months. The Second Edition was finally available for purchase at the international convention in January 2010 and was reprinted in 2017 and 2021.

> In the Second Edition, we have revised some of the original text to more clearly keep the focus on our own recovery. Several new shares have been added. All of the sharing reflects the experiences of recovering S-Anon members.

We celebrate that this Second Edition represents our progress, not perfection, as we journey together exploring the wonders of serenity, dignity, and emotional growth.

"Forward," *Working the S-Anon Program,*
2nd ed., pp. xx, xxi

When the Second Edition of *Working the S-Anon Program* was published, I quickly browsed through it and decided not to replace my first edition copy. Several years later a program friend suggested that I should replace my copy with the new edition because it contained quite a bit of new content. So, I did.

I began referring to it more often and realized that it was a hidden gem I had overlooked and underutilized. My sponsor taught me to "stay in the solution." *Working the S-Anon Program* provides me with guidance and insight on using the tools of recovery available to me. It also has become a resource used in my meeting on topic night.

S-Anon member

Reflections of Hope

In 1990, the LC discussed the idea of creating a daily meditation book written from the S-Anon point of view. They eventually began collecting writings from members in 1998. Several requests were made for new writing to be submitted. More than 200 writings had been collected by 2002, but they needed 366. They lacked volunteers to organize, review, and edit the submissions through the CAL process. Multiple projects competed for LC members' limited time. Some years passed before LC members were available to continue work on the daily reader.

This project was a huge undertaking given the number of readings and their broad range of shared experiences and topics. Drafts of the readings were sent to LC members for their review through postal mail, which also made this project very time consuming. The LC Editors worked with a member who submitted several cover designs for the book. They were excited to have a fresh, new, colorful, and creative face for our first daily reader, *Reflections of Hope*. For the first time in S-Anon Literature, an index was provided. The first printing of *Reflections of Hope* was in 2008, with additional printings in 2013 and 2020.

> I offered to be the Sponsoring Editor for *Reflections of Hope* in 2001. This was to be the most significant service project I had participated in to date. It would also prove to be a major test of my recovery. It seemed to be a race to see just how many of my defects of character could get in the way of my focus and serenity. My willingness to surrender was challenged often. I relied on my Higher Power and friends in the program, my Service Sponsor, and of course the Literature Committee.
>
> There was no precedent or road map for such an undertaking in our program. Every day I sat in front of the computer, looking at those precious words members had entrusted to us. The question I would constantly ask myself was, "How do we make sure the intent of the piece is heard?"
>
> There were countless people who contributed to this publication. Among them were Editors, Readers, and all those who submitted writings. *Reflections of Hope* was completed seven years later.
>
> Sponsoring Editor for *Reflections of Hope*

Another individual involved with the reviewing and editing process of *Reflections of Hope* shared the following:

> Before it even went to press, *Reflections of Hope* was helpful to me because I served on the Literature Committee when it was being reviewed. It was good for me to see how the process worked. I got to practice "letting go and letting God," since I didn't control what the actual outcome would be. I also got to practice using my voice to express my opinions and give suggestions for edits. I am grateful for the experience of working with the Literature Committee and seeing a long project completed.

Now that the book is published and in its second printing, I have the day June 25 bookmarked: "I Will Not Abandon Myself." I have used this reading to remind me that my boundaries are not about what the sex addict or anyone else does or doesn't do, but rather what I will or won't do. I don't have to try to control anyone else. For that I am grateful.

• • •

Up for Discussion...

1. How have I used the tools of recovery found in Working the S-Anon Program?

2. Does my group use material from Working the S-Anon Program for meeting topics? Why or why not?

3. What are some of my favorite readings in *Reflections of Hope*?

4. Does my sponsor refer me to readings in S-Anon literature when we work together?

5. Have I worked with other people to accomplish a common goal? How has my personal recovery helped the process?

6. What does "principles above personalities" mean to me when I am involved with service work?

7. How can I apply my creative expression to my S-Anon service work? Have I considered submitting any of my writing to the LC for use in future publications?

• • •

S-ANON LITERATURE IN GERMANY AND BEYOND

In the late 1980s, one of the original members of S-Anon in Karlsruhe, Germany, offered a low-cost translation of a brochure. This translation gave a brief summary of the S-Anon Twelve Steps. Printing was also arranged in Karlsruhe. By the early 1990s, the entire *S-Anon Twelve Step Study* and other literature had been translated into German. Through cooperation with S-Anon International Family Groups, Inc., in the United States, Germany now has a good selection of CAL and Service Literature available.

> This service work to create literature for S-Anon Germany was a huge endeavor for a handful of members. As a result of intensive content discussions, we were able to deepen our knowledge of the Steps and Traditions, which led to a strong sense of community. Willingness and determination have become lasting gifts from and to S-Anon Germany. We also developed our own guiding principles and recommended practices such as how to organize meetings, information, description of service work, and newsletter contributions.
>
> S-Anon member from Germany

In 1994, a Spanish translation of the *S-Anon Problem* was created by an S-Anon member in the United States who was fluent in Spanish. Several volunteers worked with the LC to complete Spanish translations of additional pamphlets. These publications became available in early 1996. Since then, our *S-Anon Twelve Steps, Working the S-Anon Program,* and several other titles were also translated into Spanish and can be purchased through the WSO website.

As interest in other translations of our literature grew, providing this literature through the WSO was no longer practical. Members in several countries have obtained a license from the WSO to translate S-Anon Literature into their own languages. When permission was granted, these members worked in cooperation with the WSO to translate and publish CAL and Service Literature. Translations now include Spanish, German, French, Polish, Slovak. Persian, Swedish, Italian, Dutch, and Hebrew.

In 2011, the LC and the BOT discussed the possibility of S-Anon literature being offered in digital format. After researching how other Twelve Step fellowships provide electronic literature and various digital book services, *Reflections of Hope* became our first eBook in 2014. Since then, electronic versions of *S-Anon Twelve Steps, S-Anon Twelve Traditions,* and *Working the S-Anon Program* have also become available in English, and some of these titles are now electronically available in Spanish.

• • •

Up for Discussion…

1. How does the realization that S-Anon extends across international borders and that our literature is available in several languages affect my perspective of S-Anon as a world-wide fellowship?

2. How has our literature in e-book format been useful to me?

• • •

S-ATEEN LITERATURE

The first teenager began attending S-Anon meetings in 1996. When teens expressed interest in attending S-Anon meetings, it soon became apparent that they could benefit from their own literature.

The original three S-Ateen members, along with two S-Anon members, drafted adaptations of the "S-Anon Meeting Format and Readings." Those adaptations were written from the S-Ateen point of view, making them more suitable for teenagers. Proposed S-Ateen readings were submitted to the LC in the fall of 1996. These readings included the "S-Ateen Twelve Steps," "Twelve Traditions," "S-Ateen Problem," "Keys to Recovery," and "Obstacles to Recovery."

In April 1997, the additional readings, "The S-Ateen Welcome," "Preamble to the Twelve Steps of S-Ateen," and the "S-Ateen Meeting

Format," were submitted to the LC. After going through the CAL process, all S-Ateen literature received final approval at the January 1998 Conference Business Meeting. The fellowship was informed that the "S-Ateen Readings" and "S-Ateen Meeting Format" were conference approved and available for sale.

In 2014, the BOT S-Ateen Committee was reactivated after being inactive for several years. They worked with the LC to produce and approve several new and updated pieces.

• • •

Up for Discussion...

1. Does my S-Anon meeting have S-Ateen literature available?

2. How might my meeting benefit from using S-Ateen literature? Have I considered sharing my S-Ateen story, if applicable?

3. If I have teenagers who might be helped by S-Ateen literature, how might I consider whether and how to appropriately share it with them?

4. If I grew up in a family impacted by sexaholism, how do I see my childhood experiences reflected in the S-Ateen Problem?

• • •

S-ANEWS
"THE MEETING YOU CAN TAKE WITH YOU"

The idea for publishing an S-Anon newsletter was introduced, discussed, and approved at the January 1989 Conference Business Meeting. Subscriptions would include four newsletters per year at an initial annual cost of $10. The first issue was provided at no charge.

> We decided to begin publication of a quarterly newsletter for the S-Anon fellowship. Our goals are to unify the membership

> and let widely scattered groups know that we are not alone. We hope that this newsletter will be a source of information for you about local meetings and about international conferences. In order for the newsletter to succeed, we need input from you! Send us news about your meetings now! Also let us know what else you would like to see.
>
> First S-Anon Newsletter, February 1989

In February 1989, the first issue of the *S-Anon Newsletter* "rolled off the presses" with rousing enthusiasm. It was two pages long and was mailed to all registered groups. The publication included a request to submit personal recovery stories. Members were asked for suggestions of names for the newsletter. An announcement was made in the second issue that the name would be "*S-Anews*."

The paid circulation started with 16 subscriptions. The newsletter became an important source of information for the fellowship. As subscriptions grew, *S-Anews* content expanded to include information about S-Anon business decisions, sharing information about individual groups, upcoming events, WSO activities, service-related items, and a few members' stories. Seventh Tradition donation figures and various fellowship-related topics were also included. News about the WSO, business decisions, the need for volunteers, and financial information is now available in the member section of the WSO website.

Some members used *S-Anews* as their meeting because they did not have face-to-face meetings in their area. *S-Anews* truly was "The meeting you can take with you," which became the subtitle of the publication. Members' stories were expanded and featured a wide range of topics.

> How I Stay Connected to My Higher Power
>
> In addition to reading, I sometimes journal, especially when I am feeling troubled. At times I write a letter to Higher Power. This helps me to clarify my thoughts and feelings and reminds me that I have someone who truly cares about me. Then I write a letter back to me from my

Higher Power. I write "I," but I ask Higher Power to inspire me and guide my pen.

The amazing thing is that I receive insights through this process that I know are not mine. I am steered into another way, a healthier way, of looking at a situation. Perspectives and solutions are presented that I never thought about. I can offer God three choices, "a, b, or c" and ask him which path I should choose. Most of the time, in the letter back, a choice "d" is offered which is far superior to my "a, b, or c."

S-Anon member, *S-Anews*, Summer 2011

The appearance of *S-Anews* changed over the years. It went from a newsletter consisting of a couple of folded pages to a booklet with a cover and multiple pages. Graphics were added. The cover went through several updates from solid color cardstock to glossy paper with color photographs.

The editorial and approval processes for *S-Anews* were not as detailed as those for CAL to provide a timely publication. While the same general criteria were used, there were fewer reviewers and less attention to detail. This newsletter was not considered CAL because it was edited by a group of LC members but did not go through the full CAL process.

Numerous rotations of *S-Anews* Managing Editors occurred during the 23 years of publication. The position was time-consuming, and it became challenging to find people willing and able to provide this service. We are grateful for the dedication of those who served. At times *S-Anews* had to be suspended or delayed due to finances, lack of writing submissions, or too few LC volunteers.

In 2012, the LC completed the spring and summer issues without an Editor. An *S-Anews* supporter came forward and offered to do the formatting. The process of collecting and editing stories required time and patience. The LC was also trying to work on several CAL projects, including a book on the S-Anon Twelve Traditions. In September the BOT decided to suspend publication of the newsletter for six months.

In June 2013, after careful consideration, it was decided to permanently discontinue publishing the *S-Anews*. Discussions weighed the resources needed to continue *S-Anews* against the benefit of using those resources to meet the fellowship's expressed need for more CAL. It was difficult to let it go, but after evaluating the pros and cons, it seemed to be the right thing to do. The Summer 2012 *S-Anews* was the last issue produced, marking the end of an era. At that time, there were 130 subscriptions at $14.00 per year.

S-Anews was an inspiring publication that many members enjoyed and appreciated. Some of the articles from members can be found in our literature and posted on our website. The WSC approved a motion in 2018 to proceed with plans for a compilation of *S-Anews* writings to be made into a CAL book.

• • •

Up for Discussion...

1. It was difficult for some members to let go of *S-Anews*. How do I determine when and how to let go of something in my own life?

2. Do I practice self-care when I am volunteering for service? How do I prioritize my time and energy? Do I have a service sponsor?

• • •

CAL AND SERVICE LITERATURE

Creating S-Anon literature has had many paths "along the journey," with occasional pauses. Throughout our history, there have been many dedicated members involved with this process. We have opportunities to participate in service to the fellowship using our life experiences and skills. Our literature has drawn us closer and helps to bring unity as we aim to put our common welfare first.

CAL is considered recovery literature. Service Literature primarily offers suggestions on how to conduct certain activities. Some examples include "Starting S-Anon Groups," "Starting an S-Anon Intergroup," and "S-Ateen: Information about Sponsorship and Meetings." Initially, there was no distinction between service and recovery literature.

Over time, efforts were made to provide a clearer distinction. The literature review process was used to make decisions about which category was more appropriate. Sometimes a piece of literature was moved to a different category, edited, rewritten, or deleted. Policies and guidelines have been developed to help members understand this process.

Today, service materials can be created by the WSO, a BOT Standing Committee, or a WSC discussion. The review and approval process is completed by the BOT and is more streamlined than the CAL process. Many service tools and materials are provided as a download at no cost.

Some Service Literature can be used to reach out to professionals such as clergy, physicians, and therapists. Professionals can learn there is a place for clients and patients to go for added support and hope. Additional S-Anon service publications provide guidance to members and groups on a variety of topics, including creating a website, the group conscience process, beyond the group level, and writing a motion.

Literature from the S-Anon point of view has helped many people. Most members find that it helps them understand the principles of S-Anon recovery and how they apply to various situations. Newcomers find help when they identify with the S-Anon problem, knowing they are no longer alone. Sharing and contributing personal experiences through writing can be healing and beneficial to members' individual recovery as well as to those with whom they share them.

We continue to expand our library of CAL and Service Literature. We trust our Higher Power as we work together to accomplish this important service work. Seeing our literature translated into other languages and made available electronically is a vision come true. Through S-Anon literature, we recover together and extend the hand of S-Anon to everyone in our global community who may need the hope and help available from our fellowship.

• • •

Up for Discussion…

1. How might becoming familiar with the CAL process as described in our *S-Anon/S-Ateen Service Manual* benefit my understanding of the service required to create our literature and the benefits of contributing to our CAL?

2. Have I shared our literature with my doctors, therapists, or clergy? Why or why not?

3. Has my group offered literature to local libraries or professional offices? What are some other ways we could use S-Anon literature for recovery and outreach?

4. Do I understand the importance of conveying a unified message in our literature?

5. How has my group used Service Literature in the past? How might we take greater advantage of Service Literature in the future?

CHAPTER SIX

Where Spiritual Principles and Business Meet: The Steps, Traditions, and Concepts

When discussing the history and development of S-Anon, it is essential to include the cornerstone upon which this program has evolved and thrived. The suggested spiritual principles found in S-Anon's Three Legacies—the S-Anon Twelve Steps, Twelve Traditions, and Twelve Concepts of Service—are the foundation of our fellowship. Members who integrate these principles into their daily lives have found them to be vital in their recovery from the negative effects of this family disease.

These guidelines have helped our trusted servants demonstrate the wisdom of the group conscience process, whether they serve at the group, local, regional, or international level. They are essential tools that have helped our program continue to grow and attract new members. When we volunteer our service, we are living examples of the spiritual awakening of Step Twelve as we strive to carry the S-Anon message and live a life based on S-Anon principles. The following is a brief look at our history of embracing these Legacies.

• • •

S-ANON TWELVE STEPS: A GUIDE TO PERSONAL RECOVERY

The S-Anon Twelve Steps are the foundation of our personal growth and recovery. The principles of the Twelve Steps are applicable to all of us, regardless of our various beliefs. Working the S-Anon Twelve Steps and practicing the principles of the Steps in our daily lives fosters our recovery from living with the effects of sexaholism in a family member or friend.

Here are the Twelve Steps we follow which are suggested for our recovery:

1. We admitted we were powerless over sexaholism—that our lives had become unmanageable.

2. Came to believe that a Power greater than ourselves could restore us to sanity.

3. Made a decision to turn our will and our lives over to the care of God *as we understood Him*.

4. Made a searching and fearless moral inventory of ourselves.

5. Admitted to God, to ourselves, and to another human being the exact nature of our wrongs.

6. Were entirely ready to have God remove all these defects of character.

7. Humbly asked Him to remove our shortcomings.

8. Made a list of all persons we had harmed, and became willing to make amends to them all.

9. Made direct amends to such people wherever possible, except when to do so would injure them or others.

10. Continued to take personal inventory and when we were wrong promptly admitted it.

11. Sought through prayer and meditation to improve our conscious contact with God *as we understood Him*, praying only for knowledge of His will for us and the power to carry that out.

12. Having had a spiritual awakening as the result of these Steps, we tried to carry this message to others, and to practice these principles in all our affairs.

(The Twelve Steps are reprinted and adapted with permission of Alcoholics Anonymous World Services, Inc. Permission to reprint and adapt the Twelve Steps does not mean that AA has approved the contents of this work, nor that AA agrees with the views expressed herein. AA is a program of recovery from alcoholism only. Use of the Twelve Steps in connection with programs which are patterned after AA, but which address other problems does not imply otherwise.)

THE TWELVE STEPS OF ALCOHOLICS ANONYMOUS

1. We admitted we were powerless over alcohol—that our lives had become unmanageable. 2. Came to believe that a Power greater than ourselves could restore us to sanity. 3. Made a decision to turn our will and our lives over to the care of God *as we understood Him*. 4. Made a searching and fearless moral inventory of ourselves. 5. Admitted to God, to ourselves, and to another human being the exact nature of our wrongs. 6. Were entirely ready to have God remove all these defects of character. 7. Humbly asked Him to remove our shortcomings. 8. Made a list of all persons we had harmed and became willing to make amends to them all. 9. Made direct amends to such people wherever possible, except when to do so would injure them or others. 10. Continued to take personal inventory and when we were wrong promptly admitted it. 11. Sought through prayer and meditation to improve our conscious contact with God *as we understood Him*, praying only for knowledge of His will for us and the power to carry that out. 12. Having had a spiritual awakening as the result of these Steps, we tried to carry this message to alcoholics, and to practice these principles in all our affairs.

Members of S-Anon are the grateful recipients of the Twelve Steps from AA. These were adapted for our S-Anon program of recovery, and many S-Anon members have found a rigorous study of the Steps to be immensely helpful.

In S-Anon's early years, we used numerous versions of the Twelve Steps and Twelve Traditions. Members substituted some of the words from AA, SA, or other Twelve Step programs to fit their perspective, and Al-Anon's Steps were the most widely used. Many groups simply replaced the words Al-Anon and alcoholism with S-Anon and sexaholism. The versions read at early convention business meetings are not known. Available records do not indicate an acceptance of the S-Anon Twelve Steps until the *S-Anon Step Study* was approved as Conference Approved Literature in January 1989.

A motion was made at the Conference Business Meeting (CBM) in January 1990 to change the wording in Step One. In many of our documents it was stated as, "We admitted that we were powerless over lust – that our lives had become unmanageable." The motion was approved to change the word "lust" to "sexaholism." This made the wording of Step One more uniform and consistent with the CAL *S-Anon Step Study*.

The Central Office received a motion in December 1990 from an S-Anon group in Colorado for consideration at the next CBM. They recommended changing what they considered to be sexist language in the S-Anon Twelve Steps, namely the use of male pronouns in reference to God. Their rationale was that the change would not affect the meaning of the Twelve Steps.

Attendees at the January 1991 CBM believed the issue was too important to be voted upon by the relatively few members who were able to attend conferences. Action on the motion was deferred until a method for taking a Fellowship-wide Group Conscience (FGC) could be adopted. The S-Anon International Committee (SIC) was asked to develop a process for conducting an FGC and present a motion at the July 1991 conference. If the method was approved, then the Colorado proposal would be the first to go through the new process.

The SIC agreed the FGC procedure would tally individual group member votes that would be counted via ballots submitted by the groups. All members would have an equal voice regardless of the size of their group. This process would also facilitate group conscience discussion and bring a broader perspective to the debate. Regional Representatives would be responsible for contacting lone members to arrange a conference call for a discussion and vote.

SIC members contacted all registered groups to verify current information and sent updates to the Central Office. A set of documents was sent to the groups explaining the purpose and process of the upcoming FGC.

A motion was approved at the July 1991 business meeting to conduct an FGC on a trial basis using the proposed method. The voting results would be reported at the next business meeting, along with recommendations as to whether the process should be permanently adopted.

The final packet for the first S-Anon FGC, which was mailed to registered groups in October 1991, explained the voting process and included a ballot to record individual member votes. A letter with the results was mailed to the fellowship in early December. Ballots were sent to 93 groups, and 30 groups responded. There were 190 individual votes: 51% in favor of changing the Steps, 43% opposed, and 6% abstained. The motion to change the language of the Twelve Steps did not pass because it failed to obtain the required approval of 75% of the members who voted.

Attendees at the January 1992 CBM agreed with the SIC recommendation to postpone adoption of the procedure used for this FGC. This was followed by approval of a motion which documented how future decisions would be made until an FGC process could be approved. A formal process for conducting an FGC has not been approved as of the copyright date of this book.

Another request to modify the S-Anon Twelve Steps was made at our first World Service Conference (WSC) in January 2004. The motion was to remove the phrase "in all our affairs" from Step Twelve and to replace it with "in all aspects of our lives." The motion did not pass; it was brought up again in 2006, and it once again failed to pass.

Members often rely on the *S-Anon/S-Ateen Service Manual (SSSM)* for guidance when presenting motions at the WSC. More information on presenting motions to the WSC can be found in Part 3 of the *SSSM*.

> Today I try to remember that the Steps are the most valuable gift I have been given. They are the roadmap to guide me as I face and deal with whatever life brings.
>
> *Reflections of Hope*, p. 46

Working with a sponsor and attending S-Anon meetings can help us understand how the Twelve Steps relate to the problem of living with the effects of sex addiction. Within our literature we find stories from members who share their experiences about developing new attitudes, keeping the focus on ourselves, healing in our relationships, finding our voice, and the gifts of service. Included are gentle reminders of how working the Steps can transform even the most difficult circumstances, inspiring a healthier way of life. Many of us on this journey have had a spiritual awakening, encouraging us to live in serenity, dignity, and emotional growth.

• • •

Up for Discussion…

1. Have I worked through the S-Anon Twelve Steps with a sponsor or sponsee? How has that experience affected me?

2. What are some examples of how I practice the spiritual principles of the Twelve Steps in my daily life?

3. How have the Steps helped me with my service commitments?

4. Have I, or has any member of my group, ever changed the wording of the Twelve Steps as read in our meeting? How could this affect the unity of the group and S-Anon as a whole?

• • •

S-ANON TWELVE TRADITIONS: A GUIDE FOR UNITY AND RESPECT

S-Anon's Twelve Traditions are principles that guide the conduct and unity of our groups. The Traditions guide the growth and health of our groups and our worldwide fellowship, just as the Twelve Steps guide our growth and our lives as individual members.

Working the S-Anon Program, 2nd ed., p. 29

1. Our common welfare should come first; personal progress for the greatest number depends upon unity.

2. For our group purpose there is but one authority—a loving God as He may express Himself in our group conscience. Our leaders are but trusted servants—they do not govern.

3. The relatives of sexaholics, when gathered together for mutual aid, may call themselves an S-Anon Family Group, provided that, as a group, they have no other affiliation. The only requirement for membership is that there be a problem of sexaholism in a relative or friend.

4. Each group should be autonomous, except in matters affecting another group or S-Anon or SA as a whole.

5. Each S-Anon Family Group has but one purpose: to help families of sexaholics. We do this by practicing the Twelve Steps of S-Anon, by encouraging and understanding our sexaholic relatives, and by welcoming and giving comfort to the families of sexaholics.

6. Our S-Anon Family Groups ought never endorse, finance, or lend our name to any outside enterprise, lest problems of money, property, and prestige divert us from our primary spiritual aim. Although a separate entity, we should always cooperate with Sexaholics Anonymous.

7. Every group ought to be fully self-supporting, declining outside contributions.

8. S-Anon Twelfth Step work should remain forever non-professional, but our service centers may employ special workers.

9. Our groups, as such, ought never be organized; but we may create service boards or committees directly responsible to those they serve.

10. The S-Anon Family Groups have no opinion on outside issues; hence our name ought never be drawn into public controversy.

11. Our public relations policy is based on attraction rather than promotion; we need always maintain personal anonymity at the level of press, radio, TV, and films. We need guard with special care the anonymity of all S-Anon and SA members.

12. Anonymity is the spiritual foundation of all our Traditions, ever reminding us to place principles above personalities.

(The Twelve Traditions reprinted and adapted with permission of Al-Anon World Service, Inc. Permission to reprint and adapt the Traditions does not imply that Al-Anon is affiliated with this program. Al-Anon is a program of recovery from the effects of alcoholism. Use of this material in conjunction with programs which are patterned after Al-Anon, but which address other problems, does not imply otherwise.)

Early records do not show the approval of specific wording for the S-Anon Twelve Traditions. At the CBM in July 1989, two motions were presented regarding the Traditions. One was approved to add the Twelve Traditions to the *Leader's Manual*. A second motion was to re-evaluate the wording and provide feedback at the next CBM.

At the CBM in January 1990, a motion was made to return

to the original AA Traditions substituting S-Anon and S-Anon Family Groups. It was suggested to keep them simple and easy to understand. After a lengthy discussion, these proposed changes were tabled so additional research could be done on some of the issues raised. The original submitting group later withdrew the motion.

The Spring 1989 *S-Anews* contained an article about using one of the Traditions to address a group issue. A call for writing submissions was made for topics describing how members applied the Traditions to their home group or how they used them in their daily lives. The goal was to use these writings to create a Traditions book comparable to the *S-Anon Twelve Steps*.

> Tradition Twelve states: "Anonymity is the spiritual foundation of all our Traditions, ever reminding us to place principles above personalities." This equality implied by "Principles above Personalities" was the opposite of the dynamic with which I grew up. I had learned not to say things that might upset someone and to adjust myself to the personality at hand. I was funny, sarcastic, angry, or quiet. I played them all very well. So, to follow this aspect of anonymity was difficult but important for me to learn.
>
> *Working the S-Anon Program,* 2nd ed., p. 44

The Central Office began receiving letters from different groups requesting guidance and clarification regarding a range of issues they were experiencing. One question related to using outside literature in S-Anon meetings, such as religious or self-help books. Clarification was also requested about restricting a meeting to women only or to other special meeting groups. Members from the SIC responded by suggesting how specific Traditions could apply to their questions. Our *Group Handbook,* which later became our *S-Anon/S-Ateen Service Manual,* provided guidance for applying our Twelve Traditions to some of those common questions. Examples were given to help groups understand the importance of using the Traditions in our service structure and in making decisions for the fellowship.

> Learning and using the Traditions has been just as important to me as learning the Steps.
>
> *Reflections of Hope*, p. 41

A letter was sent to the fellowship in the fall of 1992 announcing the CBM approval of a change to the wording in the Fifth Tradition. The second sentence now reads: "We do this by practicing the Twelve Steps of S-Anon…" instead of "We do this by practicing the Twelve Steps of SA..." After careful review of available historical documents, it is believed that this vote occurred in January 1992, at the CBM in San Diego, California.

Since then, motions to change any wording in our Traditions have come up multiple times, but none have passed. The S-Anon Twelve Traditions are often cited when various motions are presented at group, intergroup, BOT, and WSC meetings. Members have found it helpful to study how the Traditions may guide the group conscience process for motions being considered.

Many of us have studied these Traditions with a sponsor or a group. Meetings frequently include a monthly topic on a Tradition, often the Tradition number corresponding to the calendar month. We also learn how to apply these guidelines while working through issues at all levels within the fellowship. Many members have learned to apply the principles of the Twelve Traditions to other areas of their lives. The wisdom of our fellowship suggests that gaining a deeper understanding of the Traditions may result in healthier relationships with ourselves, family, friends, and coworkers. By utilizing the suggested principles found in the Traditions, we can make better choices for ourselves and connect with others in a more honest, respectful, and loving way.

> Through this act of surrender, my old "rules" have been replaced with the spiritual principles of the Steps and Traditions. I am experiencing joy—something I never thought was possible.
>
> *Reflections of Hope*, p. 27

• • •

Up for Discussion…

1. Have I studied the S-Anon Twelve Traditions with a sponsor or a study group? What did I learn from that experience?

2. Has my group considered having topic meetings on the Twelve Traditions? What has been the result?

3. How have I applied a Tradition to problems in my group or in my personal life?

4. What are some changes in me and my understanding of the Traditions since I came to S-Anon?

5. S-Anon groups that do not follow the Twelve Traditions could be less effective in helping S-Anon members recover. What is my experience with groups that have not followed the Twelve Traditions?

6. Applying the Traditions can be very helpful when facing group conflicts. How have the Traditions helped to resolve problems I have encountered in my local meeting, intergroup, or other life situations?

• • •

S-ANON TWELVE CONCEPTS OF SERVICE AND THE GENERAL WARRANTIES OF THE CONFERENCE: A GUIDE TO CONDUCTING BUSINESS

S-Anon's Twelve Concepts of Service illustrate that Twelfth Step work can be accomplished on a broad scale. The Concepts are guidelines for the World Service Office staff, the Board of Trustees, standing committees, and World Service Conference members to relate to each other and to groups.

1. The ultimate responsibility and authority for S-Anon world services belongs to the S-Anon groups.

2. The S-Anon Family Groups have delegated complete administrative and operational authority to their Conference and its service arms.

3. The Right of Decision makes effective leadership possible.

4. Participation is the key to harmony.

5. The Rights of Appeal and Petition protect minorities and assure that they be heard.

6. The Conference acknowledges the primary administrative responsibility of the Trustees.

7. The Trustees have legal rights while the rights of the Conference are traditional.

8. The Board of Trustees delegates full authority for routine management of the S-Anon headquarters to its executive committees.

9. Good personal leadership at all service levels is a necessity. In the field of World Service, the Board of Trustees assumes the primary leadership.

10. Service responsibility is balanced by carefully defined service authority and double-headed management is avoided.

11. The World Service Office is composed of an Executive Director and staff members.

12. The spiritual foundation for S-Anon's World Services is contained in The General Warranties of the Conference, Article 12 of the Charter.

THE GENERAL WARRANTIES OF THE CONFERENCE

In all proceedings the World Service Conference of S-Anon shall observe the spirit of the Traditions:

1. That only sufficient operating funds, including an ample reserve, be its prudent financial principle;

2. That no Conference member shall be placed in unqualified authority over other members;

3. That all decisions be reached by discussion, vote, and whenever possible, by unanimity;

4. That no Conference action ever be personally punitive or an incitement to public controversy;

5. That though the Conference serves S-Anon, it shall never perform any act of government; and like the fellowship of S-Anon which it serves, it shall always remain democratic in thought and action.

(The Twelve Concepts of Service reprinted and adapted with permission of Al-Anon World Service, Inc. Permission to reprint and adapt the Concepts does not imply that Al-Anon is affiliated with this program. Al-Anon is a program of recovery from the effects of alcoholism. Use of this material in conjunction with programs which are patterned after Al-Anon, but which address other problems, does not imply otherwise.)

The S-Anon Twelve Concepts of Service were adopted by the fellowship much later in our history than the Steps and Traditions. It took time for S-Anon members to understand and embrace the importance of the Concepts. We have come to see that they are essential for the health and welfare of the S-Anon program. Literature from AA and Al-Anon already was conference approved for S-Anon meetings, so S-Anon members could study the Concepts before they were officially adopted.

Starting in 1989, occasional references were made to the AA or Al-Anon Concepts of Service. They were mentioned in business meeting minutes, in some of our service literature, and in the *S-Anews*. Our *Group Handbook*, first published in 1993, used the Third Concept of AA Service when describing fellowship-wide decision making.

A recommendation was made to the SIC in December 1998, to consider changing the requirements for serving on the SIC to better reflect the growth of our fellowship. One of those proposed requirements included a commitment to study the Concepts. A suggestion was made to formally adopt the Twelve Concepts of Service into our program, but no action was taken.

Discussions took place during the next several years regarding possible changes in our service structure. Those changes were approved in 2001; the SIC became the Board of Trustees (BOT) and the World Service Conference Committee (WSCC) became a standing committee of the BOT. At that time, the BOT agreed to informally start using an adapted version of the Al-Anon Twelve Concepts of Service.

Detailed plans were finalized, and our first World Service Conference (WSC) took place in January 2004. This new service arm included the BOT members and Delegates (Area representatives selected by S-Anon groups). At that historic event, a formal vote was taken that officially approved the S-Anon Twelve Concepts of Service and The General Warranties of the Conference.

> There are many opportunities for service beyond our home group. As S-Anon grows, more opportunities to be of service become available. S-Anon's Twelve Concepts of Service (adapted from Al-Anon Family Groups, Inc.), and printed in the Introductory Pages of this book, serve as guidelines for how business is conducted in S-Anon.
>
> *Working the S-Anon Program*, 2nd ed., p. 104

Another important vote at the first WSC was to approve the S-Anon World Service Conference Charter. The introduction states it "...is a body of principles and relationships through which S-Anon as a whole can function." The Twelve Steps, Twelve Traditions, and Twelve Concepts of Service are the three legacies on which the S-Anon program of recovery stands. The Charter acknowledges that all three have equal status and that no changes can be made without written consent of three-quarters of S-Anon groups via a Fellowship-wide Group Conscience.

> Many of us work through the Steps with a sponsor. Some of us go on to study the Traditions in the same manner, but few of us know about, or have "worked," the Concepts. After I did a Traditions study, I went on to study the Concepts.
>
> I am learning many things, such as how the larger pieces of my recovery fit into service work. I am more aware of my responsibility to be more informed as an S-Anon member when doing service work.
>
> The Concepts are helping me to better understand my role as a parent, my own responsibilities and duties to others and myself, and how to incorporate my Higher Power into all my affairs. I have an obligation to the group and myself to continue to learn and then apply this knowledge, including using the wisdom of others that have gone before me.
>
> S-Anon member, *S-Anews*, Summer 2002

Since then, some groups have chosen to use the Concepts of Service as a meeting topic. Study groups have been started for those who are interested in a deeper understanding of the Concepts. When members consider taking a position on the BOT, they are asked if they are willing to study the Concepts. Service sponsors can serve as a guide through the Concepts and as a resource for facing challenges related to doing service work.

S-Anon has published only a minimal amount of literature about the Concepts. Some of our service literature refers to applying the Concepts of Service. The LC is working to add material on the Concepts to our CAL. Until S-Anon literature on the Concepts is available, members interested in a study of the Twelve Concepts can use Al-Anon and AA literature to learn how to apply the Concepts to our service work or to our personal lives. We gratefully appreciate and acknowledge the wisdom of AA's and Al-Anon's Twelve Concepts of Service.

> Some people have spent many years in Twelve Step meetings and have not actively used the Concepts. My experience is that the Concepts "fill in the gaps" and "balance" the Steps and Traditions with their emphasis on "how to do service." From early recovery, we are encouraged to do service in our group. We learn how to show up for ourselves and for others by the service we commit to doing.
>
> S-Anon member, *S-Anews,* Fall 2010

The Twelve Concepts of Service help to create structure and safeguards in which service arms can effectively cooperate and support the fellowship. Concept Twelve embodies The General Warranties of the Conference. The guidelines found in our Concepts help create an environment in which we can all work with balance, respect, and some degree of order. They give us the right and the responsibility to speak up and to listen, whether we are of the minority or the majority opinion.

The Concepts remind us of the ways our service boards are responsible to those they serve. We can accomplish our goals in a healthy manner by applying the collective experience, strength, and hope gained from running the business of a Twelve Step program. These Concepts, when followed to the best of our ability, assure us that this program of recovery is available for us and will be preserved for future generations.

> At first, I thought the Concepts were only about service, and I admit that I used them as a filter to judge other S-Anon volunteers. As a result of being deeply affected by sexaholism, I had issues with authority, and I was unable to trust. At times I believed "they" weren't doing things the right way.
>
> Eventually I learned that the Concepts created a framework for me to value myself and other trusted servants. To me,

they are a gift from my Higher Power that enables the business of S-Anon to function more efficiently. The spiritual principles found in the Concepts are teaching me how to show up and be of service in my home group, work environment, and in personal relationships.

S-Anon member

• • •

Up for Discussion…

1. Am I willing to study the S-Anon Twelve Concepts of Service with a sponsor or my group? What might be the benefits of my group devoting time to studying the Concepts?

2. What are some examples of how the Concepts have helped me to better function as part of my S-Anon group and in my daily life?

CHAPTER SEVEN

Minding Our Business

The previous chapters provided a good perspective of how S-Anon came to be an established fellowship. We heard the stories of our early members who discovered they were not alone. We learned about the evolution of public awareness regarding sex addiction. We also learned how early meetings grew, how new groups started, and how recovery events helped S-Anon members find hope and support. We saw growing unity in the fellowship as evidenced in the commitment and effort to produce our own Conference Approved Literature.

Chapter Six offered insight into how S-Anon members applied the spiritual principles found in our Steps, Traditions, and Concepts of Service when making group conscience decisions for the fellowship. Chapters Seven and Eight will show how the service structure of S-Anon developed. We will see the many stages of development of our World Service Office. Trusted servants sometimes struggled to find spiritual solutions to business concerns. Despite the challenges that came with personal recovery, many members worked hard to ensure that S-Anon would be available for those in need.

• • •

THE S-ANON OFFICE ON THE MOVE

Founding members recognized the need to have a central location in which to conduct business. The journey toward having a World Service Office took us to several states where we used a variety of spaces, including several dining room tables, a spare bedroom, and a garage. We managed with a post office box, a cardboard box, and borrowed or donated equipment. As we grew, we faced the challenge of having adequate office space, financial resources, and workers. Over the course of many years, we transitioned from a home office supported entirely by unpaid volunteers to being fully self-supporting with leased commercial office space and several paid special workers.

A small group of women established the first S-Anon business office. The historic 1983 gathering in Simi Valley, California, could be considered the first official S-Anon business meeting. Records indicate that decisions were made regarding responding to mail, setting up an office, securing representation at the next Sexaholics Anonymous recovery event, selecting literature suitable for meetings, and developing a draft of our own literature.

Two members agreed to set up the first S-Anon Central Office and in 1984 established a post office box in Phoenix, Arizona. Records indicate an S-Anon member received materials from the Phoenix office in 1984 to help her start a meeting. We do not know what materials were sent, other than "The Co-Addict Checklist." The first Chairperson of S-Anon was elected at the June 1985 Conference Business Meeting, and the Central Office was moved to her home in Oklahoma City, Oklahoma. Few details are known about the aspects of early S-Anon business.

Another founding member volunteered to work to ensure that we had a more significant role in the planning of recovery events. Early conferences were mostly considered SA events, and some SA members believed that S-Anon members were merely guests. At the end of each conference, SA members made decisions regarding future gatherings. Very few S-Anon members attended those early planning meetings, and we went along with SA's decisions. Our input and participation in recovery events continued to grow, and S-Anon eventually established conventions and other recovery events separate and independent from SA.

Many members believed that S-Anon started in early 1985 with the West Los Angeles (West LA) group but were unaware that S-Anon actually began in late 1983. In the spring of 1987, not realizing that S-Anon already had an office, the West LA group discussed the need for establishing one. After careful consideration, they agreed to operate an office. They made plans for two members to attend the upcoming conference to ask for support.

At the June 1987 conference, some SA members raised concerns about S-Anon members not doing their part at these events. They asked who was in charge of the S-Anon organization. Most attendees were surprised to learn that there was an S-Anon office in Oklahoma City. An S-Anon member from West Los Angeles expressed frustration that the needs of her local groups were not being met. She said that the West LA group was willing to take responsibility for the office but did not want to make decisions on behalf of the fellowship.

Discussions from that meeting resulted in the idea of having elected representation. The minutes stated, "We would ultimately like to have elected representatives from each Region as liaison to the Central Office. However, right now volunteers are welcome from different areas with at least one year in a Twelve Step program." Attendees agreed that S-Anon groups would provide financial support for the office through Seventh Tradition contributions. Other revenue sources included sales from literature and *S-Anews* subscriptions.

After the June 1987 conference, the S-Anon Chairperson in Oklahoma City agreed to send the office material to Los Angeles. Members of the West LA group waited with anticipation for the arrival of the "office." A short time later, a *single* cardboard box of papers containing all the S-Anon business records arrived.

Soon after the West LA group received the box, *Dear Abby* contacted S-Anon. This syndicated advice column was planning to publish a letter from someone needing help because of their spouse's sexual behavior. They wanted to know if S-Anon would be prepared for the mail we might receive. This gave the West LA group the incentive to become more organized. They obtained a post office box, and an answering machine was set up in the garage of a member's home.

Once the article was published, more than 150 letters and calls were received. The workload quickly became too much for the Los Angeles volunteers to manage. At the December 1987 CBM, approval was given to hire a secretary. Hired in January 1988, she was the first paid office worker, and she worked five hours per week. Two members volunteered to help oversee her work.

I was actually the first hired employee of the S-Anon office. My bosses were my sponsor and one other S-Anon member. Later, a team of S-Anon members from around the country was developed and became the central point for procedures and literature. It worked out perfectly for me because I could stay home with my toddler. I worked while he was sleeping. I took him with me to the UPS store and the post office. The office itself started in my dining room and later moved to my garage. I had a desk, a typewriter, and a filing cabinet. When I took a vacation, my sponsor filled in as the secretary.

First S-Anon paid worker, Office Secretary

• • •

BECOMING TRUSTED SERVANTS

Once the decision was made to hire our first paid employee, we gave greater attention to the need for Seventh Tradition contributions. Members began to understand the wisdom of Tradition Seven, which states: "Every group ought to be fully self-supporting, declining outside contributions." Beginning in 1988, we encouraged attendees at conventions and other recovery events to ask their home groups to send Seventh Tradition contributions to the S-Anon Central Office.

In late 1988, four members from different local areas volunteered to function as liaison to the Central Office and help with administrative business decisions. They were known as the Central Office Committee (COC) and served temporarily until the S-Anon International Committee (SIC) was established in early 1989. Decisions on bigger issues would still be made at Conference Business Meetings where all attendees could have input.

The first conference call meeting of the COC took place in December 1988. They discussed the upcoming conference and the agenda for the business meeting that would be held the following month. The initial meeting of this committee is the first record of S-Anon business being conducted via conference call rather than in person. (All S-Anon business meetings previously had been face-to-face and took place at the national conferences.)

At the January 1989 conference in Salt Lake City, Utah, the COC Secretary gave a report to the fellowship regarding the office. The *S-Anews* publication provided financial information, summarized office activities, and reminded members of the need for Seventh Tradition contributions. Groups and members responded generously and proceeds from the July conference were used to support the office. Although some months reflected a negative cash flow, at the end of the year, we had a small net balance.

Members made important fellowship decisions at that January 1989 CBM. They presented and approved guidelines for an SIC. The SIC would consist of four to six members who had at least two years in the S-Anon program. Members of the committee would oversee routine S-Anon business and work with the Central Office Secretary to provide much-needed assistance and direction. The SIC would conduct regular business meetings by conference call.

Each SIC member would serve in a specific capacity. The Treasurer would keep track of all expenditures and monies collected. The Correspondence Liaison would keep track of incoming and outgoing mail, phone inquiries, and handle public relations. The Conference Coordinator would be the liaison between the previous and the next conference and assist with event planning. The Literature Coordinator would keep track of which pieces of literature had been Conference Approved and which were not. They would oversee the writing, printing, and distribution of new literature.

The SIC proposed a rotation schedule of these new positions along with a suggestion to create four to six geographic Regions. The goal was to improve communication among groups, as well as between Regions and the Office. Each Region would nominate a member to serve on the SIC. Those proposals were approved as well as two additional motions: 1) to change the name of the fellowship to *S-Anon International Family Groups*, and 2) to change the name from Central Office to *S-Anon International Office*. Although the second motion passed, the office name change was seldom used.

After the January 1989 business meeting, a letter was sent to known groups and lone members and was printed in *S-Anews*. The letter explained the new SIC service structure and called for volunteers to fill the service positions. The second and final conference call for the Central Office Committee occurred in May 1989. No one else had volunteered; therefore, members who had previously offered to serve on the SIC selection committee agreed to fill the four SIC positions. The formation of the SIC was a major step in S-Anon's development.

> We would have a conference call and talk about the issues that would come up. I used to type the minutes while we talked on the phone and then I mailed them out the next day. Looking back, it was unbelievable what we were able to accomplish on our conference calls without a computer or Internet.
>
> Early SIC member

• • •

Up for Discussion...

1. Do I understand the responsibilities of the WSO? How do I stay informed about their activities?

2. Does my group make routine contributions to support the WSO and the services it provides to our fellowship? What are some ways we can do that?

3. Am I willing to consider service work? While doing service work in S-Anon, how do I balance it with self-care?

4. What have I learned from my S-Anon service that has helped improve my personal relationships?

• • •

THE SIC GETS TO WORK

The newly formed SIC had its first conference call on June 20, 1989. The workload for both the SIC and the Central Office grew quickly. Members passed a motion at the following business meeting to increase the secretary's time to 20 hours per week. The secretary used the additional hours to support the SIC's effort to develop CAL. Two new members volunteered to join the SIC. One began work on establishing Regions and having elected representation. The other agreed to help with literature.

The S-Anon Central Office received a letter in the fall of 1989 from SA concerning the S-Anon logo. An excerpt from the letter follows:

> You may not be aware that our logo is trademarked and thus protected in the same way our registered copyrights protect the literature. It has been called to our attention that our logo appears on much of your literature. As you tell us you are in the process of revising your literature, we felt this might be a good time to bring this to your attention.

Questions about our logo were thoroughly discussed at the January 1990 CBM. We decided to leave our logo as is and respond with a letter explaining our position. (Throughout our history, the S-Anon logo has changed several times to better represent our ever-changing fellowship.)

> To SA headquarters:
>
> February 5, 1990
>
> We were a little confused by your letter dated October 17, 1989, which stated, "It has been called to our attention that our logo appears on much of your literature." We were unaware that we were using the SA logo on any of our literature.
>
> We have carefully looked through all our literature and have not found the SA logo on any S-Anon literature. It was

> thought that perhaps you were referring to the similarities in the two logos (SA and S-Anon).
>
> This item was on the agenda of the Business Meeting in Nashville and after some discussion, it was decided unanimously that we would keep the S-Anon logo as it is. In this decision, we are following the traditions of AA and Al-Anon, whose logos are similar, yet different. For reference, we have enclosed pictures of the four logos.
>
> Our intent is that our logo be distinctive, although somewhat similar to, the SA logo. We feel that we are all suffering from the effects of the same disease in our lives—that disease being sex addiction.
>
> Thank you for bringing this to our attention so that we can discuss it. We are currently in the process of putting copyrights on our materials, also.
>
> S-Anon member, *S-Anews*, Winter 1990

The SIC spent a great deal of time trying to address financial issues. Although the Central Office still responded to every inquiry, they reduced the number of materials sent to inquirers. They made changes to the phone line to reduce costs. The Central Office could not print the updated Step Study because of insufficient funds. Some members loaned money to the Central Office to print and ship the January 1990 convention literature. The Central Office Secretary delayed her pay and shortened her hours to help the situation.

The SIC saw a connection between literature sales and the financial state of the fellowship. The following was part of an update given to attendees at the January 1990 CBM:

> As the program grows, our ability to produce income becomes crucial. We discovered that members and groups are making copies of the literature we sell.
>
> A revenue generator for the office is its ability to sell S-Anon Literature. It is important that literature is not copied but that it is purchased from the office. The more literature that is bought, the more S-Anon is served.

The fellowship responded, and by the following month, our bank balance increased slightly. Finances continued to be troublesome. In May 1990, an S-Anon member requested permission to provide the literature for the upcoming conference by making copies. This member would send any money made from literature sales to the Central Office. The SIC agreed since there wasn't enough money to pay for printing and shipping. The conference sent Seventh Tradition Contributions collected for S-Anon to support the Central Office.

The S-Anon Central Office Secretary had difficulty trying to maintain an office in her home and sent a letter to the SIC in May 1990. The following are excerpts from that letter:

> I would like to move the Central Office into my garage where there is much more room. This would help ensure anonymity of the fellowship as it is getting more difficult to transfer S-Anon materials from room to room when we have visitors come into our home.
>
> I do have a volunteer willing to provide labor for free and propose that S-Anon pay for the materials needed to convert the garage. I believe the cost would be $600 including a 15% discount.
>
> 1990 Central Office file

Until then no rent had been paid to conduct S-Anon business. After lengthy discussions, a motion was approved at the July 1990 CBM to pay $600 rent for S-Anon's previous use of the secretary's home. Attendees concluded that this decision was consistent with S-Anon's Seventh Tradition. The secretary used the money to make modifications to the garage, and then moved the office there.

As S-Anon continued to grow, so did our business needs. The desire to obtain non-profit status became a strong motivation for some of the work done by the SIC. In 1990, they developed incorporation documents necessary for S-Anon to become a non-profit organization.

Local groups began speaking up about issues important to them and submitting motions for consideration at the CBM. The SIC created guidelines to help members when writing and submitting motions. They distributed a business agenda to registered groups ahead of each conference. They established guidelines to use during the business meetings, which resulted in a more efficient process.

The work accomplished by the SIC in 1990 helped S-Anon gain solid footing as a Twelve-Step organization. We began to transition to a service structure filled with a group of volunteers who were better able to address the requests and needs of our members.

• • •

Up for Discussion…

1. Does my group buy and sell only CAL? Do I understand the value of CAL and how its sale supports the WSO and S-Anon as a whole?

2. Can I give an example of "letting go" and trusting that needs will be taken care of by my Higher Power in service work or in my personal life?

• • •

PROGRESS, NOT PERFECTION

Participants at the January 1991 CBM discussed five motions related to changes in how to conduct S-Anon business. Members approved all five motions, including the "S-Anon Statement of Purpose" and the "S-Anon Preamble to the Twelve Steps."

Six Regions were established based on the number of known registered groups in the United States and Canada. Each Region would have a representative on the SIC. Approval for anyone who volunteered to represent a region could be voted on either at a CBM, if practical, or by the SIC. S-Anon would follow this procedure until a regional election process was established for each Region. A motion passed that identified the requirements to serve on the SIC.

Members on the SIC agreed to represent a Region during the transition. They became known as Regional Representatives and would serve a three-year term as voting members of the SIC. Many times, the outgoing Regional Representative recommended a member as their replacement.

When changes to the S-Anon legal service structure were approved in 2001, the SIC became the Board of Trustees (BOT) and the Regional Representatives became Regional Trustees. As group organization and Regions developed and grew, some Regions approved a process to elect their Regional Trustee. The Regional Trustees are voting members of the BOT and serve as a valuable resource to groups, intergroups, and Area Delegates. When a Delegate position is unfilled, the Regional Trustee can serve as liaison between groups in their Region and the BOT, to provide groups with a voice concerning issues in the fellowship.

> I had the strange sensation of watching myself from a distance as I raised my hand at the annual World Service Conference to volunteer to serve on the S-Anon Board of Trustees. I felt willing to serve, and I knew I had the time available, but almost immediately I began to doubt that I really had anything of value to offer, and to fear that somehow my S-Anon program and I would not be good enough. This was not a new feeling—often these same doubts and fears had kept me from getting involved in activities-- but I have discovered that the safest, most supportive way for me to confront these fears and move past them is to participate in S-Anon service work.
>
> *Working the S-Anon Program*, 2nd ed., p. 106

Another appeal was made to the fellowship in the spring of 1991, for needed office equipment:

> We are in the process of updating the International Office. We receive and respond to more than 100 letters a month. We organize the *S-Anews*, distribute material to the LC, and perform a number of office tasks. We have grown to the point where it is necessary to buy some office equipment

> to expedite this work. We are currently using a borrowed desk. We have one used file cabinet and last year we purchased a typewriter.

The Central Office Secretary resigned her position in July 1991. The SIC discussed options for relocating the office and began looking for a small space to rent and a new employee. To keep business running as smoothly as possible, we temporarily moved the Central Office to the home of the acting Office Administrator.

We hired a new part-time secretary, and a member volunteered to work with her to track finances, balance our accounts, and keep financial records current. The part-time secretary soon resigned, and the Office Administrator filled this paid part-time secretary position. Business liability insurance was required to lease commercial property, which S-Anon could not afford. As a result, the Central Office remained in the Office Administrator's home in southern California for several years.

> We decided that the Chicago area groups were going to work toward a goal of buying a fax machine or some piece of equipment for the S-Anon office. I had always pictured a sleek, glass California office building. Once I saw a photo of the secretary's office, my perspective radically changed. It is exciting to see where our donations would be going.
>
> S-Anon member, *S-Anews*, Winter 1992–1993

As attendance at international conventions increased, groups experienced some confusion about procedures for hosting these events. The SIC determined that written guidelines could help. They approved the first set of Convention Guidelines in December 1991, and they have been revised several times since. S-Anon groups that hosted a local or regional event or International Convention found the guidelines to be helpful.

The Central Office was not receiving bank statements in a timely manner, which made it difficult to manage our finances. The SIC recognized the importance of keeping better financial records to help make decisions. Beginning in 1992, the SIC received a simple monthly financial report. While it was useful, the SIC struggled to cover our bills and to decide on financial priorities each month.

The SIC often discussed ideas for raising money to support the Central Office. They mailed a seven-page letter to all registered groups in May 1992 to raise awareness of needed funds. This letter described how the office supported the fellowship and provided details on expenses and sources of income for the first quarter. Included were questions for groups to consider, as well as a list of suggestions as to how individual meetings could increase financial contributions.

In another effort to encourage financial support for the Central Office, the Fall 1992 issue of *S-Anews* contained an article about fund-raising events held by the Los Angeles area groups. These included several successful S-Anon fellowship potluck dinners and other events.

The SIC established our first budget in 1993. A volunteer set up a spreadsheet that provided more thorough financial details. Setting up a budget and having routine financial reports helped track income and expenses. We were better able to make informed decisions about our priorities.

Publication of *S-Anews* was turned over to volunteers instead of using our paid staff. This reduced expenses and allowed the SIC to spend more time on other business matters. The SIC appointed an Office Oversight Committee to review the Central Office functions and expenses and consider ways to reduce overhead. The committee made steady progress toward improving our financial situation.

Detailed job descriptions, including job tasks, which were established by the SIC in 1993, helped to streamline office operations. As additional time became available, the SIC was able to put more effort toward long-range planning.

It is worth noting that a significant event occurred on December 7, 1993. After years of effort, S-Anon International Family Groups finally became incorporated, and in December 1996, received non-profit status.

• • •

Up for Discussion…

1. In what ways, from both a financial and service perspective, does my group support an intergroup, Area Delegate, or Regional Trustee?

2. Does my group make decisions based on a group conscience? What might be the benefits of this?

3. What does an informed group conscience mean to me? How can I apply that to my personal life?

4. How do I support my group, and S-Anon as a whole, to help fulfill our primary spiritual aim?

5. How can I become aware of how my financial contributions are being allocated to various service arms?

6. How do I understand Tradition Seven as it applies to my S-Anon group, S-Anon as a whole, and my personal life?

CHAPTER EIGHT

Practicing These Principles

The S-Anon story recounts the many challenges we faced while taking care of business for our fellowship. Similar to our individual journey in recovery, our S-Anon fellowship has worked through conflicts, misunderstandings, and challenges. We are grateful to members who were willing to work to find solutions. The fellowship has continued to grow and be available to those seeking help; this could not have happened without those who were willing to serve. Learning how to apply the suggested spiritual principles from the S-Anon Steps, Traditions, and Concepts of Service takes time and patience.

> I am constantly amazed how the skills I've learned in serving the S-Anon fellowship touch every part of my life. Had I not taken on that first bit of service work in the accepting environment of S-Anon, I would not have grown as I have.
>
> S-Anon member, *S-Anews*, Summer 2003

• • •

THE MOVE TO NASHVILLE, TENNESSE: EXPERIENCING NEW GROWING PAINS

The S-Anon Central Office initially operated out of private homes in Arizona, Oklahoma, and California. In May 1994, the Central Office Administrator in California informed the S-Anon International Committee (SIC) of her pending move to another state. The SIC discussed possible locations for the S-Anon headquarters. Nashville, Tennessee, had several S-Anon meetings whose local members expressed a desire to support the Central Office. After lengthy deliberations, the SIC members voted unanimously to accept their offer and relocate to Nashville.

Sexaholics Anonymous was also moving its office to Nashville and offered S-Anon part of its space and use of office equipment for $100 per month. Our finances were limited, so the SIC accepted their generous offer without anticipating the possible consequences. A special committee of three Nashville members was appointed to coordinate moving the office. A local member agreed to fill the position of General Secretary as a contract employee on a temporary basis.

The Nashville Intergroup generously provided $400 in seed money, and by early December a new phone number, post office box, and bank account were established. Once the move was completed, the SIC appointed a new Central Office Oversight Committee that would provide regular reports to the SIC on issues concerning the office. S-Anon *finally* had a commercial location after years of using space in members' homes.

Within a short period of time, the Oversight Committee was presented with a new set of challenges. To reduce the amount of foot traffic and address privacy concerns, SA requested that S-Anon limit the number of volunteers coming into the office and that they not have office keys. A few months later, S-Anon was asked to separate our office space from SA's, so that S-Anon volunteers would not need to walk through SA's space. By the end of 1995, we were able to pay our secretary for additional hours, which reduced the number of necessary volunteers and solved the problem.

Although the office relocation was a major effort, the SIC continued to work on several other projects such as literature, conferences, and conference guidelines. The SIC also received detailed financial reports that aided them in making financial decisions. S-Anon broke even for most of 1995 and started to see a small surplus toward the end of the year.

In early 1996, we began paying our special workers as S-Anon employees instead of contract workers. We developed a budget and cash flow improved, which allowed S-Anon to purchase its first computer. With the help of the Oversight Committee and careful use of available funds, our finances remained reasonably stable for the next few years. Increased Seventh Tradition donations and literature sales were indications that S-Anon was growing.

As the Internet became more widely used, the SIC realized that an S-Anon website could be a vital way to carry the message of S-Anon recovery and provide member information resources. In 1997 the SIC reviewed options for establishing a home page on the Internet. They agreed to register a nonprofit ".org" domain address, and in the spirit of "Keep it simple," chose www.sanon.org. The website went live in late June. Soon after that, members started raising questions concerning linking our website to other sites. The SIC (and later the BOT) addressed each request individually until a formal policy for website links was developed many years later.

In the summer of 1997, we were notified of a sizable rent increase. This prompted us to look for office space elsewhere. S-Anon moved into our first independent office in early October. Many members considered this a milestone for the fellowship and another important step toward becoming fully self-supporting (Tradition Seven).

As finances improved, business decisions became less stressful, and the Central Office was better able to address problems in a timely manner. Some initiatives included setting up a Speakers' Pool, creating new policies concerning children and teens at conferences, establishing a network for long-distance sponsorship, developing a media kit, and improving the process for filling SIC positions.

When the office moved to Tennessee, it became necessary to dissolve the previous corporation, incorporate in Tennessee, and acquire a new tax ID number. In 2000 S-Anon hired an attorney to help us become established in Tennessee as a nonprofit organization. By-laws were required to outline matters regarding elections, terms of office, and responsibilities for our trusted servants, including Officers and a Board of Trustees. The SIC began working on the necessary documents.

Early in 2001, the S-Anon office received some inappropriate and threatening phone calls. The office contacted a few members of the Oversight Committee and the SIC. To address safety concerns, they quickly moved the office to a suburb of Nashville and changed the mailing address and phone number. Since only a few members had been part of the decision to relocate, the SIC discussed the decision at length the following month. Some SIC members were unaware of the events that led to the move and were concerned about the impact that this rushed decision would have on S-Anon as a whole.

Many SIC members, who met via conference call, believed that this decision was not made by an informed group conscience, which would be appropriate for such an important and sensitive action. Securing the office manager's safety and moving the Central Office were discussed as two separate issues, and the SIC members agreed that there were other ways to have addressed the problems. In hindsight, they concluded that holding an emergency meeting would have allowed all members to provide their input.

The SIC scheduled an additional meeting to address what would be in the best interest of the fellowship and the office staff. The issue was not resolved in the special meeting. The SIC agreed to take time to seek Higher Power's guidance and resume discussion at the next regularly scheduled meeting.

By June of 2001, the Office Administrator and two Oversight Committee members resigned. To assure continued service to the fellowship, the SIC approved a motion to hire the Southern Regional Representative as acting Office Administrator.

During another special meeting, the SIC agreed to move the Central Office back to Nashville and resume using the original Nashville post office box mailing address and phone number. Our new office space was larger. Both the building and office suite required a key for entry, which provided greater security.

In addition to finding solutions for important office issues, the SIC continued to work on the by-laws and update the way S-Anon conducted business. A special three-day face-to-face meeting was held in Nashville in August 2001 to change the service structure. Current and former SIC members attended. The weekend was very productive, and the participants approved a new business model similar to the one used by Al-Anon.

A three-page letter dated September 18, 2001, was mailed to groups outlining the new service structure and associated terminology. The S-Anon International Committee (SIC) became the S-Anon Board of Trustees (BOT), and the Central Office became the World Service Office (WSO). The letter explained the creation of seven standing committees: Executive, Budget, Literature, International Convention, Delegate Conference, Public Information, and Archives.

Regional Representatives became Regional Trustees on the BOT. The Delegate Conference Committee was charged with developing plans to create a Delegate Conference (now known as the World Service Conference) wherein the fellowship at large would be represented, and larger issues would be addressed in a more formal process than at the Conference Business Meetings.

The year 2001 ended with a deficit greater than $16,000, following a year that had surplus funds exceeding $11,000. S-Anon's financial situation was greatly impacted by the disruption of the Central Office. This included two costly moves of the Central Office and the associated telephone conference call meetings. The special face-to-face reorganization meeting in Nashville and a decrease in Seventh Tradition donations were contributing factors.

• • •

Up for Discussion...

1. How can people seeking S-Anon recovery find our meeting? Does my group keep the WSO up to date on changes such as a new contact person, a new meeting, disbanding of a meeting, or changes to meeting location, day, or time?

2. How do I seek information when I have questions about S-Anon business or procedures? Have I ever accessed the S-Anon website or contacted the WSO?

3. How has S-Anon helped me to accept that at times there will be disagreement?

4. Can I express myself without having to defend how I am feeling?

5. Am I able to listen to others with an open mind and carefully consider what they have to say?

6. Do I regularly attend my group's business meetings? Does my group consider everyone's opinion during a group conscience process?

7. Does my group consider the possible impacts its decisions and actions may have on S-Anon as a whole?

• • •

A NEW SERVICE STRUCTURE

The restructuring of S-Anon was a seven-year effort stemming from a need to reincorporate in Tennessee and register as a non-profit. After reorganization was approved by the SIC, there were many decisions to make before moving forward. The new BOT adopted by-laws outlining how business would be conducted. Six existing SIC members filled the four officer positions and the chairperson positions for the Literature and Convention Committees.

The Regional Trustees accepted an additional role of "Acting Chairpersons" for the remaining committees until volunteers were found and approved. All Chairpersons agreed to serve one three-year term. Information about this new structure was sent to groups, posted on our website, and published in *S-Anews*. The BOT asked members to consider volunteering to fill the vacant positions. Some positions were filled quickly; others were not. A few committees remained inactive for several years. The new Committee Chairpersons looked for members to serve on their committees.

Operating expenses increased because of a larger service board. Financial support for each committee was added to the budget as they requested funds for their proposed work. A special appeal for donations was made to the fellowship in early 2002.

> The World Service Office (WSO) is currently experiencing a substantial budgetary shortfall and is requesting members and groups to consider an increase in their financial support. Costs have increased significantly; please consider increasing your financial donations if you are able.

> The WSO provides the unity upon which personal progress for the greatest number depends. It does this by sponsoring regular conference calls of the Board of Trustees and its Committees, and by providing all registered S-Anon groups with current fellowship updates, literature information, and voting ballots.
>
> And last but not least, the WSO supports the efforts of the Committees of the Board of Trustees, through which our fellowship is able to have an appropriate service structure to address the needs of our members, publish and update our body of literature, and provide financial oversight of the WSO, to name only a few of many functions. Thank you for your support!
>
> WSO Special Appeal, 2002

The Board continued to look for ways to reduce expenses and implemented quarterly (later became triannual) special appeals to ask members to contribute additional funds to the fellowship if they could. The financial situation worsened through 2002. Costs to cover conference calls and operating expenses increased due to the newly formed committees. Other expenditures included computer replacement and new accounting software. We also experienced a decline in literature sales and Seventh Tradition contributions.

We continued to finalize details of the restructuring and organizing of BOT committees. The BOT decided that a yearly Delegate Conference would be held prior to each January international convention beginning in January 2004. This replaced the semiannual Conference Business Meeting. The name of the Delegate Conference Committee was changed to the World Service Conference Committee, and the annual Delegate Conference became the World Service Conference.

The World Service Office had difficulty hiring staff from the local Nashville S-Anon membership, and volunteers were unable to provide adequate support. Events from the previous two years resulted in disagreements among some of the Nashville members, and financial struggles added stress to the problem. In the fall of 2002, BOT members began to talk once again about moving the WSO out of Nashville.

In March 2003, the BOT held another special face-to-face meeting in Nashville to complete details of the restructuring. While there, the Board met with local S-Anon members to discuss challenges they were experiencing with the WSO and the Trustees. They identified several problems, and everyone agreed to continue the discussions until acceptable solutions were found.

The BOT began planning to relocate the WSO due to lack of available candidates to fill office positions and lack of local support. The BOT sent notification of the pending move to the intergroups. Members were asked to consider moving the WSO to their area if there were enough qualified members and volunteers to run the office. By the end of 2003, the choices were narrowed down to Los Angeles and Detroit, but no decisions were made at that time.

During 2004, BOT members continued to work with local Nashville members to find possible solutions for issues regarding the office. Progress was slow but steady. By August, the local groups offered their willingness to support the office if it stayed in Nashville. The BOT approved a motion at the following meeting that the WSO would remain in Nashville.

In addition to working through critical office issues, the BOT looked for ways to encourage the growth of our Area Delegate body. Four letters were sent to S-Anon groups during 2003. The first letter described the World Service Conference (WSC) and explained its purpose. It announced the date and location of the planned WSC. While all S-Anon members were welcome to attend the meetings as observers, the voting members included Delegates from each Area, the six Regional Trustees, the BOT Standing Committee Chairpersons, the four BOT officers, and the WSO Executive Director.

The second letter invited the Area Delegates and groups to submit motions to the WSC and provided a motion submission form. The third letter continued to encourage Areas to send a Delegate to the WSC and included an Area Delegate registration form. The final letter was sent only to registered Area Delegates and included a WSC packet with all the motions and a business agenda for the upcoming WSC. This packet clarified that based on the BOT By-laws, the BOT Standing Committee Chairpersons were Trustees-at-Large and voting members of the WSC. The S-Ateen Committee was also identified as one of the standing committees.

It was a difficult and challenging time for many members who were involved during this stage of our history. At times emotions ran high and tested members' patience and their commitment to finding solutions. Using the spiritual principles of the S-Anon program, the fellowship emerged as a stronger organization and has continued to grow.

• • •

Up for Discussion…

1. Does my group hold regular business meetings and encourage participation? Why or why not?

2. Have I ever attended the S-Anon World Service Conference? What was my experience?

3. How do my emotions affect my decisions?

4. What group conscience decisions did I disagree with at first, but later grew to appreciate?

5. What does my group do to support our service boards such as intergroups, Delegates, Regional Trustees, standing committees, or the BOT?

• • •

THE WORLD SERVICE CONFERENCE

The first World Service Conference (WSC) took place January 9, 2004, in San Diego, California, the day before the international convention started. Twenty-eight World Service Conference members attended the first WSC. Ten motions were considered. Four of these motions were approved: adopting the Twelve Concepts of

Service adapted from Al-Anon, adopting the World Service Conference Charter, adopting the BOT By-laws, and approving the slate of Trustees for the next year. Having a Delegate body as part of the process provided a better way for groups to express their wants and needs in matters affecting the fellowship. S-Anon seemed to be ready for this new way of conducting business. Two members who attended the first WSC shared their experience in *S-Anews*.

> On January 9, 2004, I attended the first ever S-Anon World Service Conference in San Diego, California. From my viewpoint, a Higher Power's presence was certainly guiding the process of the meeting. Throughout the four-hour meeting various motions were presented, discussed, and voted on. What I experienced was an amazing process. Some debates on the motions came with strong opinions on both sides of the issue. To the fellowship's credit, debates were heard with open minds and respectful attitudes.
>
> WSC Delegate, *S-Anews*, Spring 2004

> S-Anon's Twelve Concepts of Service were formally adopted at the first WSC. Concept Four, "Participation is the key to harmony," was the theme that was echoing in the room for me that day. I was and still am amazed at how the process works. I felt honored to have been a member of this WSC.
>
> BOT Trustee-at-Large, *S-Anews*, Spring 2004

At the completion of their initial three-year terms, all the BOT Officer and Trustee positions ended, and few people came forward to fill these vacancies. Many of the retiring Board members volunteered to continue on the BOT and shifted to different positions. Three of the Committee Chairperson positions remained vacant.

As they gained experience, BOT members adjusted some of the business processes. In early 2005, the Budget Committee became the Finance Committee to better reflect its responsibilities. Later that year, the decision was made to stagger the terms of Officers and Trustees for smoother BOT functioning and to avoid having a board comprised completely of new members. During this time, an ad hoc committee of current and former BOT members began working to revise the *Group Handbook*. The revised service structure and policies were included, as well as the meeting format and questions raised by the fellowship. This document became the *S-Anon/S-Ateen Service Manual (SSSM)*, first published in 2007.

After the first WSC, attendance by Delegates remained low. Overall attendance at international conventions in July was noticeably higher than at the January conventions. The BOT voted to move the WSC to July, beginning in 2008, hoping to improve participation.

Until 2009, the Delegates met at the annual WSC with little prior planning and organization. Establishing a system of Area representation was a huge undertaking. They struggled among themselves with how to best proceed. The Delegates were challenged to define their role with their local groups as well as how they would interact with the Board.

The BOT discussed how they might be of help. The Board turned to the Concepts of Service for guidance to communicate with the Delegates. Careful attention was given to Concept Seven: "The Trustees have legal rights while the rights of the Conference are traditional." Consideration was given to Concept Ten for guidance on how to balance service authority and avoid double-headed management.

The BOT suggested making a monthly conference call line available for the Delegates to conduct business. This could support efforts to set up a communication network, define responsibilities, and recruit additional Delegates. In turn, this would strengthen the Delegate body's commitment to represent the voice of the fellowship.

To assist the Delegates, the Trustees agreed the WSO would cover the cost of monthly conference calls for six months. The first conference call was on September 20, 2009, and included a few BOT members to answer questions. The following year, the Delegates held an Assembly just prior to the WSC. Since then, their representation has grown in both strength and numbers.

> I volunteered to serve as Delegate in an Area that wasn't represented. My motivation was simple. As a person with a tendency to isolate, I know that I am safest when I am actively engaged in healthy amounts of service. For me, healthy service puts me in the "center of the herd" and surrounds

me with recovering people. Some people are ahead of me on the path; some are behind. Service at the Delegate level makes my herd much bigger.

S-Anon member, *S-Anews*, Spring 2011

The BOT struggled with an increasing workload and looked for ways to become more efficient. Policy-related questions were taking up a lot of time at monthly meetings, which led to the creation of the Policy Committee. Establishment of the Policy and Service Communications Committee was approved in August 2009. The BOT also recognized the need to improve communication among its service arms. They considered the roles of the Regional Trustees and Delegates and developed better descriptions of their responsibilities.

A problem occurred with the WSO office space in 2009. A hair salon moved into the adjacent space and strong chemical odors permeated the office. The Administrative Assistant became ill and resigned her position. The Office Administrator was also affected by the odors, so she began to work from home when possible.

The office struggled to keep up with the workload. The relationship among the BOT, the Executive Committee, and the WSO staff became strained. Our commitment to the spiritual principles of the program helped us find solutions. We broke our lease, secured new office space in a nearby building, and moved the office in December 2009.

The S-Anon service structure has components that include both legal and traditional aspects. As part of the Traditional service structure, members represent their Area groups. As part of the legal structure members serve on the Board of Trustees or on one of the BOT Standing Committees. This is explained in Part Two of the *S-Anon/S-Ateen Service Manual*. As a Twelve Step fellowship, we must satisfy our business obligations while honoring our Legacies. Service arms address the needs of S-Anon members and develop ways to do outreach, while maintaining good financial stewardship. The wisdom in our Twelve Traditions and Twelve Concepts of Service guides us in maintaining financial stability.

• • •

Up for Discussion…

1. Does my group understand the S-Anon service structure and the difference between traditional and legal aspects?

2. In what ways do I or my group give input to S-Anon decision making at the intergroup, Area, Regional, or international level?

3. Am I able to voice my opinion in S-Anon and in my personal life and let go of the outcome? Do I accept group conscience decisions?

4. How do I rely on the Twelve Traditions and Concepts of Service to keep my emotions out of group conscience discussions when stating my opinion?

5. Our first General Warranty from the S-Anon Twelve Concepts of Service suggests S-Anon include an ample reserve as a prudent financial principle. How can I apply this to my personal life?

• • •

BEING OF SERVICE IN S-ANON

Soon after walking into an S-Anon meeting, we begin to hear how important service work is for our personal recovery and the welfare of our fellowship. Getting involved in service helps us develop confidence. Many of our readings and meeting topics teach us that being of service is one of the gifts of the program. It is a way of giving back what we have been given.

It is helpful to know that we do not have to be perfect to be of service. Decisions are made based on group consensus; no member's voice is more important than another's, and no one member has authority over the fellowship. Contrary to many of our experiences before recovery, we learn to work together by listening and sharing our opinions. Other ways for us to practice our program include volunteering, working with a sponsor, sponsoring others, learning about the Traditions and Concepts of Service, and utilizing slogans.

There are several service opportunities within our local groups: setting up chairs before a meeting, being keeper of the room key, or serving as treasurer or secretary. Even at a group level, most service positions come with a time limit known as "rotation of service," which is determined by each meeting's group conscience. Rotation of service allows all members the opportunity to serve and ensures a steady flow of new ideas that help us follow the spiritual principles of our program.

Later in our recovery, we learn that there are opportunities to become a trusted servant beyond the group level. At special events such as marathons or conventions, help is usually needed with registration or literature, leading a breakout session, or being a speaker. Some groups coordinate to set up an intergroup responsible to the groups it serves. Each group has a representative with a voice and a vote who participates in the intergroup. Other positions could include serving as an Area Delegate, a Regional Trustee, a member of the BOT, or as a member of a BOT committee.

> As I've worked through some Steps with a sponsor, I am aware of how important service is. If it weren't for someone deciding in the past to start a meeting, I wouldn't have a group to go to. If someone hadn't manned a phone line, I would never have found my first meeting.
>
> I can give back by doing service work. It only takes as much time as I'm willing to spend, and I get so much more in return. Our fellowship always has opportunities for me to help others (and myself in turn). Today I pray for my Higher Power to turn my eternal gratitude into the willingness to serve a fellowship that has so generously and anonymously endowed me with a real and beautiful life.
>
> S-Anon member, *S-Anews*, Summer 2004

S-Anon has often had too few members doing the work of many, and sometimes positions have remained unfilled for long periods of time. This puts even more strain on our trusted servants. Being of service can be rewarding, but also time consuming, stressful, or frustrating. Finding solutions to business issues among a group of people with differing ideas and personalities can challenge our serenity and our commitment. Members who volunteer their time should consider finding balance, being mindful of self-care, and setting boundaries. Service sponsors can help us work through these issues.

Challenges may occur concerning a group's organization and procedures. Members may consider themselves "leader of a group," because they started that meeting or do not believe anyone else can do the job as well as they can. Other times, a group might view a member as an expert and think that they have all the answers, but no one member has all the answers for a group. This is why business meetings and a group conscience are so important for discussing group matters.

Conflict can occur when a member fills multiple roles at the same time. Rotation of leadership is an important tool to prevent conflict in local meetings and beyond the group level. When a member's service term ends, someone else has an opportunity to volunteer. This creates a space for others to use their skills or develop new ones. By following rotation of service guidelines, more members have a chance to be of service and affirm their sense of belonging. Service work can help us stay committed to our program and strengthen our recovery.

Other ways to find solutions for concerns or conflicts include talking with our sponsor or another member or contacting our Area Delegate or Regional Trustee. We can also refer to the *S-Anon/S-Ateen Service Manual* or other S-Anon Service Literature for helpful suggestions.

Some members participate in study groups about the Traditions and the Concepts of Service. Meeting topics about service and the role of leadership are often helpful. Group conflict issues should be raised and discussed at business meetings, hopefully resulting in resolution of the problem by a group conscience.

When we work through situations as they occur, we go forward reminded of our common welfare and unity, as stated in Tradition One. Tradition Two reminds us that "Our leaders are but trusted servants; they do not govern." Our Concepts of Service and General Warranties of the Conference are also useful.

We learn how to work through difficult situations even though we are an imperfect group of recovering people. Both our mistakes and our successes have helped us to apply the principles of recovery in all areas of our lives.

This is not the end of our journey. As S-Anon continues its primary purpose to help those affected by another's sexual behavior, there will be new problems to solve, new obstacles to overcome, and new decisions to make. We trust that our members will discover the "Gifts of the S-Anon Program" and continue to have the courage to work through each situation...*Along the Journey.*

• • •

Up for Discussion...

1. When I do S-Anon service work, how has the slogan "First Things First" helped me to practice self-care or set boundaries?

2. What positive experiences have I gained from volunteering for service, either in my group or beyond the group level? How has service impacted my recovery?

3. How does my group encourage newer members to become involved in service?

4. What do I find to be the most challenging aspects of service?

5. Why have I hesitated to volunteer for a service position? Am I afraid of making a mistake? Have I considered talking about my fears with my sponsor or other S-Anon members?

6. What is the role of a service sponsor? Am I open to having and working with a service sponsor? Am I willing to be a service sponsor?

7. How has a service sponsor helped me work through a difficult issue?

INDEX